MASHPEE NINE

Center of Mashpee, 1976

The Pond

Boat Landing

Twelve
Acres

Down
Street

Fire Barn
Ockry's
The Corner

Legion

Collins
Lot

Main St.

Mother's
Lounge

Mill
Pond

Mashpee River

Up Street

Town
Hall

Police
Station

MASHPEE
NINE

A STORY OF
Cultural Justice

PAULA PETERS

SmokeSygnals

2017

This book is published as a companion to the documentary
short film *Mashpee Nine: The Beat Goes On.*

SmokeSygnals
25 Devon Street
Mashpee, MA 02649
smokesygnals.com

Second Edition

Printed in the United States of America

Edited by Julie Lipkin

Illustrated by Robert Peters

Designed by Greta Sibley, gretasibley.com

ISBN 978-0-9976289-1-3

DEDICATED IN MEMORY OF

LEWIS "LEW" GURWITZ

— HIS ENDOWMENT FOR

FUTURE GENERATIONS OF WAMPANOAG

Anticipating the next note, beaters poised over the drum.
(Photo by Russ Price)

P8hp8hwuneek[*]

The Drum

In the space between Mother Earth, Grandfather Sky, and Creation, the Drum moves.

The Wind is the river upon which our conversation travels; the Drum, our constant sacred companion, carries our prayers along this river.

From the soul, to the mind, to the hand, to the Drum and out to All . . . flows our history and hopes carried by our beloved: our Drum.

In the still soft places where the mysteries of the Universe are kept, the Ancestors await word from us. Our breath rides upon the soft waves of the Drum, who carries our lessons of life back to our place of origin in the Universe; the Drum lays there our song and prayer at the feet of Creation.

—*jessie little doe baird*

---

* In Wôpanâak (the Wampanoag language) 8 represents a long "oo" sound.

Acknowledgments

This effort would not have been possible without the patience, tolerance and unconditional love of my husband, Mark, and my family — too expansive to list by name. To the Nine and the Mashpee community, I thank you for being so generous with your stories.

I also need to acknowledge the Mashpee Wampanoag Tribe Archives, the Mashpee Historical Commission, the Mashpee Public Library, the *Cape Cod Times* and *The Falmouth Enterprise,* and reference librarian Faith Lee at the Falmouth Public Library, who never tired of my ineptitude with the microfilm reader.

Thank you Mother Bear and Rachel Carey Harper for believing in this story and inspiring so many others to care.

Special thanks to my transcriber, Rhiannon, my photo editor Steven, and to my mother for saving every damn news article ever written about the Tribe.

Thanks also go to my readers Judy Shapiro, Hana Doe Bernadett, Lisa Lambert Nicholson, Ann Gilmore, and my proofreader Glena Bendure, all brave enough to be both critic and advocate and sharp enough to find typos Julie and I had become completely blind to in the end.

And last, because everyone's story matters, I am grateful to Bob Costa and Woggy for their stones. Without them there would be no balance.

July 29, 1976, 12:30 A.M.

The canvas flap ripped open with a violent tug. An intruder shoved his way inside, cutting the darkness with blinding beams of light, kicking gear, shoving the sleeping men and shouting, "Get up! Move!"

Twenty-one-year-old Lincoln Hendricks was stunned. "Who? What the . . . ? Damn!"

He jumped up and bolted out of the tent into the clearing by the fireside to see one of his cousins lying in the dirt, hands cuffed behind his back. A cop in riot gear — helmet, vest, shield — ran toward Lincoln with a black baton raised over his head.

The darkness of that moonless night would be his friend as he ran in the direction of a path his feet would have found even if he'd been blind.

Earlier that day a large group of Mashpee Wampanoag family and friends had gathered at that same location — Twelve Acres — for a feast. It was by all accounts an impromptu celebration, part of a budding cultural revival that had included a successful pow-wow earlier in the month, a cultural camp for tribal children and work done to recreate a 17th-century-style tribal village on the hill overlooking Mashpee Pond. The village, funded by a federal grant, had become a focal point of pride for the Tribe, providing a renewed sense of identity connected with history. Tribal youths attending the summer camp conducted on the same site were witnessing the village springing up like a garden of the Three Sisters: corn, beans and squash. And like the vegetables that nourished their bodies, the village nourished their cultural appetite.

Lincoln was among about a dozen or so tribal men involved in the construction of the village who had attended the daylong celebration.

As the sun went down, the gathering waned and families with children went home, while others stayed into the evening for drumming and singing by the fireside. There was still quite a bit of food, including fresh-caught fish, chowder and batter for fritters. Some brought spirits to drink, but the focus remained communal and festive. By the time the singing was done, all but about a dozen men had gone home. Lincoln, exhausted, had just retired into a tent where tools and supplies for the children's camp were stored. The camp director had gotten a permit to allow a few of the men to stay in the tent and provide security for the site and the supplies.

Lincoln lay down and was just drifting off to sleep. A few men remained at the fire talking. The drumming had stopped and the crackling fire and a chorus of crickets were the only sounds to be heard before all hell broke loose.

Now Lincoln tore down the dark path toward the town landing. He could hear shouting, screaming, dogs barking aggressively. It was pure chaos. Lincoln couldn't imagine what had provoked it. From the landing he circled back to his grandmother's house behind Ockry's Trading Post. He ran inside and found his hunting rifle and loaded it.

"I had never in my whole life grabbed a gun to use against people — only for hunting," he said, recalling the horror of that night. "I felt like I was getting a gun to defend my people. That had never happened before."

Armed for battle, his heart banging in his chest, Lincoln crept through the woods from his grandmother's house, crossed behind the back of the fire barn to the edge of the American Legion Hall parking lot where he could see but remain unseen. There were more police in riot gear standing guard over several more of his cuffed cousins, illuminated by flashing blue lights of several police cars. Police in marked cruisers raced up and down Main Street in a frenzy, enforcing a new kind of law no one had seen coming.

At that moment, common sense overruled Lincoln's sense of fear and desperation; it was clear there was nothing one man with one rifle could or should do. He lowered his gun and stepped back into the shadows.

A decade of change

As the civil rights movement was being waged in cities across the nation, few Mashpee folk had televisions to keep up with the drama. The isolation of the seaside village had a *Secret Garden* aura that both insulated and inured the residents to the rest of the world.

Tribal member Robert Allan Maxim recalls growing up in Mashpee in the 1960s and learning to appreciate the rural quality of the town and the abundant natural resources both in terms of recreation and sustenance. In those days every young man had a rifle and a quahog rake and learned free-range hunting — for game of all sorts in the Mashpee woodlands, and for shellfish in the many bays along the shoreline.

"Those were the best times of my life," recalled Allan, called by his middle name among Tribe members and in the Mashpee community. He matured to become a man who would become a key player in both Tribe and town politics.

The Mashpee school went only to the sixth grade, after which students were farmed out to neighboring towns to be educated. Allan graduated from Lawrence High School in Falmouth in June of 1969. In the fall he left for Oklahoma, where he earned an associate's degree from Bacone College, established in 1880 to educate Native Americans. By the time he returned to Mashpee in 1973, much of the lifestyle he'd known and loved in his hometown had changed. As a young tribal member with a sheepskin on his wall, Allan was quickly recruited to serve on the newly established Mashpee Wampanoag Tribal Council, developed to preserve what was left of the Tribe's homeland and maintain the Tribe's culture and heritage. The Council was also tasked with addressing a particular injustice occurring in Mashpee, one similar to what city dwellers were experiencing.

With the 1960s had come the emergence of gentrification, a phenomenon made more palatable when described as "urban renewal" in places like Boston's South End and Bay Village. Taking run-down brownstones and developing them into highly valued homes, with little or no consideration for families who had lived there for generations, was lauded by city planners. While the fancy term "gentrification" was certainly not in the nomenclature of the typical Cape Codder, the effect was palpable in Mashpee with sudden growth, land loss and encroachments on a tribal lifestyle that had endured there for centuries. Instead of blue-collar families being pushed out of brownstones, as in Boston and other cities, it was tribal families who were losing control of their town in Mashpee; the critical social and environmental habitat that sustained them culturally, financially and, ultimately, politically was being eroded at an alarming rate. Not knowing what to do, folks stepped around the issue like a moose in the parlor. But that moose was about to kick over a lantern.

In July of 1976 a 15-year-old Mashpee Wampanoag boy was filled with a sense of rage that had its roots in personal and cultural conflict he was far too young to comprehend. He wasn't born with it, but he certainly had come by it honestly.

Between 1965 and 1975, the decade when "the Boy" had grown from a toddler to a teenager, the territory where his Tribe had endured for centuries experienced a dramatic change. It happened so fast; the rural town that had been an idyllic indigenous paradise by tribal standards became a seaside suburb seemingly over-night. A statewide building boom hit so hard that Mashpee was singled out as the fastest-growing town in the commonwealth of Massachusetts.

The Boy was part of a large Wampanoag family and, like most tribal youngsters, rarely traveled far from home — even more rarely across the canal on either of two bridges that connect Cape Cod to the mainland. Mashpee was both a homeland and a sanctuary where his siblings, extended family of cousins, aunts, uncles and tribal relatives created a social and cultural safety net.

His early years had been marked by all the simplicity a tribal life on Cape Cod could offer. As soon as he could walk his tiny feet had earned calluses barefooting over shell driveways, woodland paths, cracked tar and dirt roads. If he wasn't pedaling one of a few shared bicycles, running was his primary mode of transportation; like most Wampanoag children, he had learned to be fast or miss out on something fun — or, worse yet, be caught engaging in some kind of mischief. He would run from home to Samuel G. Davis School, to Collins' Lot, to Ockry's Trading Post, and to the fire barn, where the mostly volunteer firefighters were called upon on rare occasions for anything of an official nature. There was a good chance he would interrupt a game of bid whist and the firefighters would shoo him off: "Too hot out, boy, git on down the pond!"

Then he might divert across Main Street to Mother's Lounge and peer inside to see his mom and dad seated at a table made steady by a book of matches tucked under one leg. They would typically be enjoying some stuffed quahogs while tipping tall-neck bottles of Schlitz, laughing and sharing stories with other folks. If he was lucky, his parents would have a few extra pennies and he would double back to Ockry's and press his face up to the glass candy display and point to his favorites. Elwood would stuff the candy in a tiny brown paper bag, often including an extra Tootsie Roll or jawbreaker. Then the Boy would dash down a narrow dirt path and over a small hill to Mashpee Pond, where he would share his stash.

Summer days were especially cherished, even as they began at the crack of dawn for most Mashpee folk. Men left the house for the bay, toting fishing gear, as women got out to hang laundry and tend gardens before heading off to clean fancy homes in Osterville or Hyannis Port. By noon most everyone was free to cool off in the pristine waters of Mashpee Pond and stretch out on the beach, where families picnicked and kept an eye on bare-naked toddlers as the older children stripped down to their underdrawers and T-shirts to go swimming. Actual swimsuits were a commodity few could afford when getting wet was all that mattered.

The lifestyle must have seemed frivolous, even lazy, to newcomers, who understood little about the Wampanoag taking guilt-free advantage of well-earned leisure time and enjoying a relatively simple life.

And the seemingly unguarded children roaming the town must have been an even bigger mystery to those new to Mashpee. But truth be known, whether they were "Down Street," as the east end of Main Street was defined, or "Up Street," where the west end hooked sharply upward to the north, "down on the Corner" (pronounced Cornah) where Great Neck Road met Main Street, or on Mashpee Pond, Wampanoag children were always in their back yard: They were secure under the watchful eye of a vigilant tribal community that was the equivalent of a chain-link fence with an attack dog on a long lead.

The Boy would hardly have recognized the wave of modern colonization cresting over Mashpee in the early 1960s. It was subtle at first, but about to crash like a tsunami.

Lured by the beat of the drum

Willard "Billy" Pocknett had worked all day and had missed the feast at Mashpee Pond. Later that night he was at a friend's house for a bid whist party. The card game was a popular pastime among Tribe members, who were fiercely competitive but played for little more than bragging rights at the American Legion Hall. When the game ended, Billy headed home.

"We only had one car at the time and my wife had it, so I was walking home," said Billy, who was coming from Down Street to his Up Street home. Rounding the bend at the mill pond he recalled, "I could hear the drum. It wasn't loud. It was nice, and I could see the flicker in the sky from the fire.

"So I headed on up there, where I knew the guys were up there drumming. They asked me if I wanted something to eat and I sat down and just started talking. That's how I ended up there that night."

As in many indigenous societies, the drum, often referred to as the heartbeat of the people, is the social, cultural and spiritual center of the Mashpee Wampanoag. In the early '70s the tradition was strengthening among the Wampanoag men, who held regular sessions to practice old songs and learn new ones.

A group of men circled the drum, pounding in unison with long sticks — beaters — crafted of dowels or sections of retired fishing poles and padded and wrapped at the end with deer hide. Some beaters were decorated at the handle end with bright colors and fringe. The men chanted, straining their voices to the highest pitch, veins bulging in their necks, sweat dripping from their faces. Some singers cupped a hand to one ear singling out their tone from the voices of the others. It was late so the songs had become more social:

If you'll be my honey,
I will be your sugar pie oh aye ho!
Whey ya hey aye ho,
Whey ya hey aye ho!

A missed beat here and there and cracked voices were signs it was time for the singing to end, and several folks went on home, but Billy stayed. He recalls sitting there just talking by the fire for some time before he saw lights approaching through the trees.

"I noticed lights coming through the woods . . . and I could hear dogs," Billy said. He wondered if some of the guys had organized a raccoon hunt without telling him. "I said, 'What the devil? Are they out coon hunting tonight or what?' And then I saw they were coming from all angles."

Several of the men at the fireside began to scatter, but Billy sat right where he was as several armed officers emerged on the scene.

"Only reason I stayed is because I knew I hadn't done anything wrong," he said. "I was the first one arrested."

As he was being cuffed and thrown to the ground, he asked what he was being charged with.

"Disturbing the peace!" the cop told him, then whacked Billy hard on the shoulder with his nightstick and told him to shut up.

From that point on Billy had what he described as a "ringside seat" to the raid.

"I was watching them chase the guys through the woods . . . . Of course, my guys, they all scattered when they saw the riot gear, the helmets, the big shields; they had the dogs on leashes, nightsticks . . . . I said, 'What in the devil is going on?' I could not believe it!"

The building boom

If Billy Pocknett had a ringside seat to the raid on Twelve Acres, Allan Maxim was in the front row for the building boom that exploded in Mashpee in the 1970s.

"The early 1960s to 1970s were really wonderful times," Allan recalled. "Mashpee was, for the most part, relatively undeveloped."

With large tracts of forested land and unblemished estuaries, rivers and lakes, Mashpee was a hunting and fishing paradise — both for seasonal sportsmen, for whom it was purely recreational, and for tribal families, many of whom drew their primary sustenance from the woodlands and waterways.

But that lifestyle was being threatened. As Allan recalled, "Mashpee was right on the precipice of probably the most explosive development and growth period in New England's history."

The state census verifies the staggering transformation of Mashpee between 1965 and 1975. In a just a decade, the year-round population grew by 300 percent, from 665 to 2,500.

A landscape once dotted with modest homes and barns, farmlands, smokehouses and fishing boats was being transformed at an astounding rate. While Up Street and Down Street managed to maintain the tribal community character, the rest of the town was becoming obscured by neighborhoods and strip malls that sprang up across deer runs and blocked access to shellfish beds. Newcomers built fences and posted signs making ancient ways into private roads.

"In about the early '70s we saw the emergence of probably the most renowned community development on the East Coast when the New Seabury Corporation took about 2,000 acres of south Mashpee that abuts Vineyard Sound," Allan recalled of the resort community for wealthy retirees that served their recreational interests, including boating, golf and tennis. "Suddenly there was an interest in this town that had been pretty much avoided."

Not only did New Seabury take an interest; the corporation took advantage by filing a petition in state land court to abandon all ancient ways to Jehu Pond within the development. Legal notice of the filing was missed by both the town and Tribe until it was too late. The land court had already approved the measure privatizing trails the Tribe had used to access the pond, saltwater estuaries and the ocean for fetching eel and shellfishing for generations. In March of 1974 Mashpee Wampanoag Tribal Council President Russell Peters took the matter to the Mashpee selectmen, demanding to know how such a thing could have happened. An attorney for the New Seabury Corporation said the land court had sent notification of the intent to Mashpee selectmen and had received no response. Selectmen denied having received the letter.*

Wearing hand-me-downs and his signature smile, the Boy walked with his brothers and sisters to the Samuel G. Davis School, where new kids arrived on buses looking as if they'd just stepped out of the Sears Roebuck catalog and carrying tin lunchboxes embossed with cartoon characters. The Boy had difficulty learning and had developed a reputation for being a bit of a rascal as his frustration with classwork manifested itself in clowning around, to the amusement of his classmates.

His mother was not amused. She encouraged her

---

*Staff contributor not noted, "Tribal Council objects to loss of ancient ways to New Seabury," *Falmouth Enterprise*, March 29, 1974.

Boy to do better. A self-proclaimed "mama's boy," he made his best effort on her behalf, and it was soon reflected in an uptick in his grades and promising reports from his teachers.

But the Boy's mama was not well, and at the age of 11 he lost her. She had been sick for some time, but it had never occurred to him she would die. The shock of the loss caused him unthinkable grief, and even in the midst of a large family and Tribe, he felt alone with it. He admits he just stopped caring about school. Nothing made sense anymore.

By that time the parents of those Sears Roebuck kids with the clanging lunch pails were running the Town Hall that had once been dominated by Tribe members. Nonnatives filled elective offices and police cruisers, and became wardens of one kind or another. Newcomers were leading Mashpee in a direction unfamiliar and uncomfortable to the tribal community.

The growth phenomenon was noted benignly in the 1964 Mashpee Annual Report: "The population is still on the increase and many fine people are coming to the Town to live, permanently, as well as the many who are attracted by our natural resources—the seashore and fine summer weather," the Board of Selectmen wrote.

By 1965 that "unprecedented growth" had been identified as a "building boom," though still considered a manageable sign of the times ameliorated by "the installation of a central switchboard to be manned 24 hours a day" for calls to the town's police and fire departments. Town Hall was also opened for recreational activities like basketball practice and supervised roller-skating. In 1967 the town's first shopping center opened at what is now Mashpee Commons, providing more than 100 jobs: "Development continues at a rapid pace in New Seabury, John's Pond and Santuit Pond areas," the selectmen's 1967 report stated.

As these reports were released, the unanticipated result of tribal disenfranchisement among town leadership had yet to be realized. The town's three-member Board of Selectmen, administrative offices and police and fire departments were still dominated by members of the Tribe and tribal spouses. Tribe and town issues were essentially one and the same. People just assumed it would stay that way. But it didn't. And by 1970 the new mix of citizenry was being felt in officialdom.

Not only were new town leaders not Wampanoag, they also drove a new kind of economic engine through Mashpee that rolled right over tribal values.

"The selectmen at the time, they were all builders. Everyone had a development going somewhere in town," Billy said. "The town was growing, and there was a lot of tension between the Tribe and the town."

When deeded to the Wampanoag in 1665 in a Colonial act that promised the land to the "South Sea Indians" forever, Mashpee was originally called a plantation. It was established as a sanctuary for praying Indians. But centuries of encroachment, coercion and manipulation exposed the Mashpee plantation — the Colonial equivalent of a reservation — to a calculated kind of vulnerability. First at the hands of greedy overseers, who leased woodlots to neighboring plantations for the purpose of clear-cutting trees for fuel in the 18th century, and ultimately for all-out land grabs in the 19th century, when it became clear the Wampanoag would not be viable for a "Trail of Tears"-type of removal from desirable land.

Despite the centuries-old promise and a federal law prohibiting the sale of Indian land, township was forced upon the Tribe in 1870, with deeds instantly granted to naive Tribe members who had no concept of land ownership or the responsibilities that came with it. Many could not even read.

In the century post-township, hundreds of acres of tribally owned land were sold or lost, often to pay debts or to satisfy back taxes, particularly during the Depression. Despite that dramatic change in land ownership to include many nonnatives, most of whom built summer camps on the lakes and seashore, Mashpee retained its small-village character. The Wampanoag lived there in a kind of comfortable obscurity that preserved them as a distinct community. There were both known and invisible boundaries and unique customs and societal structure universally understood among the Natives, yet confounding and ambiguous to outsiders. That all changed with the dramatic surge in population, which seemed to coincide with the election of President John F. Kennedy and the establishment of the Kennedy dynasty's "Camelot" in the neighboring village of Hyannis Port.

So instead of coming for respite with canoes and fishing poles, nonnatives came with moving vans filled with all their worldly goods. They came to stay and, unlike the seasonal folk content with the simple pleasures of Mashpee, these new neighbors wanted progress and profit, two advantages that involved the exploitation of land and resources and infringed on the very lifestyle of the Wampanoag. It became clear to Tribe members that, should the trend be allowed to continue unchallenged, they would be forced out of their homeland as the mill workers had been evicted from Back Bay to make room for the gentrified.

But what could they do? Newcomers had already assumed leadership roles previously dominated by Natives, who no longer had the votes to maintain their hold on critical elected positions.

So in 1972 the Wampanoag began holding meetings in the basement of the Mashpee Baptist Church to organize and develop strategies for maintaining the Tribe's foothold in Mashpee. Order was established under Robert's Rules, bylaws were hashed out and officers elected to the newly established Mashpee Wampanoag Tribal Council. By 1974 the bylaws were established and the organization incorporated with a not-for-profit 501(c)(3) status.

The Tribal Council established a government arm to the tribal body, filling the void in leadership that town officers once provided. The Tribal Council operated separately, but with regard for the cultural arm of the Tribe, fully engaged in a revival that reinforced the Wampanoag heritage and ancestral connection to Mashpee. The interconnectedness was illustrated by the relationship between the brothers Russell "Fast Turtle" Peters, who became the first Tribal Council President, and John "Slow Turtle" Peters, the Tribe's Supreme Medicine Man.

In the 1950s a contemporary of the Peters brothers, Earl "Flying Eagle" Mills Sr., had been named Tribal Chief. As Earl Mills he taught physical education in the Falmouth Public Schools, but as Chief Flying Eagle he reinvigorated tribal traditions honoring the earth, nature and four directions in a more formal way. The annual homecoming event, begun in the early part of the century as a tribal reunion, became an official powwow in a cultural sense under Chief Flying Eagle. His wife, Shirley Mills, took great pride in raising their four children to honor and respect their heritage. The children were taught to perform a Four Winds dance to honor the north, east, south and west.

"We raised our kids in the Indian way, really," Shirley said. "At the powwows the four little ones would dance, they would do the Four Winds — that was really something to see, because they were shy . . . . But that is how they started out on the powwow trail."

The Cape Cod town became a cultural mecca for New England tribes, who flocked to the annual Mashpee Wampanoag Powwow each July and to traditional social gatherings scheduled throughout the year, with drumming and dancing. Intertribal trips were organized for Wampanoag youths to visit other Native communities.

Nonnatives were often surprised about the behaviors of the Mashpee originals; they were commonly heard to utter the phrase "oh my gosh!" — particularly at the sight of unclothed children splashing in the pond, or a hunter stringing up a bleeding buck from a tree branch in front of his home. As a result, the outsiders became known among Tribe members as "Goshes" — not by any means in a threatening or insulting way, but in a traditional sense. It was a nickname earned by a behavior exhibited almost universally by the nonnative newcomers and associated with the expression "oh my gosh."

As the newcomers began to assume more and more authority over the customs and doings of the Wampanoag in Mashpee, most notably hunting and fishing, the Tribal Council began to respond.

Among the original missions of the Tribal Council was a determination to reopen ancient ways obscured by the New Seabury Corporation and other developments. Neighborhoods, a golf course and opulent homes with grand landscapes were developing with no regard for the public access Tribe members had used for centuries to reach the ocean, bays and estuaries for fishing.

After the Tribe raised the issue of gaining legal access to ancient ways, in some cases the rights of way were restored. Other ancient ways, including those wiped out by the land court within the New Seabury development, remain blocked to this day.

New homeowners were largely content to stay neutral on the matter of Tribe/town relations, while some found benefit in the cultural enrichment and historical significance the Tribe gave the town. To commemorate the town's centennial in 1970, signs had been crafted welcoming people to Mashpee with the words "Land of the Wampanoag" engraved symbolically on an overlaid plaque in the shape of a primitive arrowhead.

Assuming the colorful Natives to be an otherwise harmless source of cultural enrichment to their burgeoning community, the new establishment in Mashpee turned over the dilapidated Avant homestead across from the parsonage on Main Street to be restored as a museum of tribal history just before the centennial. Amelia Peters Bingham, chairwoman of the Mashpee Historical Commission and a vocal tribal advocate, successfully lobbied the federal government for funds to restore the house. Mrs. Bingham was named the director of the Wampanoag Indian Museum of Mashpee.

There was growth, but there were still vast amounts of open space in Mashpee, and the Tribe found a few allies among conservationists and those interested in protecting land in its natural state; wildlife habitats and the relatively novel idea of historic preservation were taking hold. In the spring of 1975, Tribal Council President Peters advanced a request to town meeting on behalf of the Tribe for the town to turn over a large parcel off of Great Neck Road South to be used for traditional gatherings and, ultimately, to build a tribal headquarters. It was approved.* In keeping with a

---

* Town of Mashpee Annual Report, 1975.

trend of sorts, it was called by its approximate size, Fifty-Five Acres. (Some years later the site was formally engineered and determined to be closer to 58 acres, but the name stuck.) A ceremonial clearing was soon after developed in the middle of the property, but if the townsfolk assumed the Tribe would disappear into that wooded lot, they were sadly mistaken.

From South Cape Beach to Punkhorn Point to Ashumet Pond and Mashpee Pond, the Tribe was developing an emboldened sense of entitlement, in the face of phenomenal residential growth and development, to exist just as it had for hundreds of years. Tribe members hunted, fished and camped, but not without challenges to their livelihood and basic sustenance when newcomers landscaped over access roads and staked claim to private beaches. Support for staking the Tribe's access claims came in the form of legal help from the Native American Rights Fund sending fledgling attorneys to advise the Tribe of its rights and avenues to pursue justice. By the summer of 1976 the Tribe and town were engaged in a delicate dance of decorum, barely missing one another's toes.

In the center of the dance the Boy quietly cried himself to sleep, missing his mother. He dreaded the end of summer and returning to school, where his experience was marked by failure. He was hurt, offended and angry and didn't know why. His path in life was fraught with challenges, change and loss. Conformity was not in his vocabulary, and he resisted authority of every kind.

Tactical control

The phenomenon of growth was not exclusive to Mashpee on Cape Cod. All 15 towns were experiencing an extraordinary level of new construction, forcing them to revisit overall governance from a local and county level for matters such as zoning and water protection bylaws and the adequacy of infrastructure. Despite the obvious interconnectedness of the towns' shorelines, bays and estuaries, and the marshlands, forests and rare wildlife habitats that made the region so unique, it would be decades before the Cape Cod Commission Act was passed to provide regional oversight to manage development. However, a unique law enforcement collaborative was created far ahead of the curve.

In 1970, Massachusetts State Police and officers from most of the Cape's 15 police departments began to engage in militia-style drills in a Barnstable County-funded program called the Cape Cod Tactical Patrol Force (CCTPF). The early model of a Special Weapons and Tactics team (SWAT) received state and county funding to amass an arsenal of equipment including shields, helmets and weapons. In addition to more sophisticated guns, they acquired clubs, mace and specially trained dogs specifically for the purpose of containing unruly crowds and riots. They even acquired a patrol wagon to haul away the most stubborn degenerates. The problem was that unruly crowds and stubborn degenerates eluded the CCTPF.*

While the crime rate on Cape Cod saw an increase commensurate with the population growth in the early '70s, it hardly even

___

* Staff contributor not noted, "Tactical force shows its stuff," *Falmouth Enterprise,* July 6, 1976.

warranted a full-time district attorney, and the courthouse was still served by circuit judges from other counties.

Despite the relatively quiet rural lifestyle on the picturesque peninsula, the post-Vietnam-era commandos of the CCTPF were literally outfitted for war. And the fiscal 1976 state budget included $5,000 for even more equipment and training.

A village on Twelve Acres

Mrs. Bingham had a vision for the Wampanoag museum that extended beyond the quaint historic house on Route 130. Engaging her grant-writing skills once again, she wrote a detailed proposal for more federal funds to build a small village of 17th-century-style dwellings on land behind the museum along the Mashpee River.

In January of 1976 Mrs. Bingham's proposal was funded by the U.S. Office of Economic Opportunity's Community Service Agency. The federal grant, in the amount of $68,400, was awarded to the town of Mashpee for the purpose of developing an outdoor living-history exhibit, a 17th-century Wampanoag village including a longhouse, a single-family wetu and a lean-to made of cedar saplings, fire pits for cooking and warming, drying racks, a wolf trap, a traditional garden for growing corn, beans and squash, and a garden watchtower.*

But it nearly didn't happen. A rift had developed between the Mashpee selectmen and Mrs. Bingham. In particular, Mrs. Bingham and Selectman George Benway did not see eye to eye on where to locate the outdoor historic exhibit. Mrs. Bingham had written the grant with the expressed intention of building the

---

* Town of Mashpee Annual Report, 1976.

exhibit on property across the street from the museum; Benway insisted it needed to be on tribally owned property 5 miles away, in South Mashpee. The only Wampanoag on the three-member Board of Selectmen, Frank Hicks, was a lame duck to his two white fellow board members, Benway and Kevin O'Connell. As part of an effort to reorganize and modernize town government, the full-time position of town administrative secretary had been created, and Mr. Hicks had been hired to fill it but would vacate his selectman seat in the next election.

The board dismissed Mrs. Bingham.

"They locked me out of my museum," she recalled.

As the town struggled to fill the director position at the museum, the Tribe rallied to preserve the selectman seat vacated by Mr. Hicks with a Native candidate. Tribal Council Vice President Allan Maxim was considered the best hope and, in what was considered the town's most competitive election, Allan joined the board in May of 1976.

One of Selectman Maxim's first challenges was to prevent his fellow board members from returning the $68,400 grant to the federal government for lack of an administrator. Allan agreed to take on the responsibility to oversee the grant.

He was also able to persuade selectmen to allow the exhibit to be developed as intended on 12 acres that included an old overgrown ball field in Attaquin Park overlooking Mashpee Pond. The parcel, known as Twelve Acres, was just a short walk from the Mashpee Wampanoag Museum, allowing for programs to be connected.

In June about a dozen men were hired to clear the land, harvest cedar saplings and develop the exhibit. Down in South Mashpee they waded into the swamp area at Fifty-Five Acres to collect cedar poles; coming up short, they sent a crew of half a dozen men to a swamp in Vermont to get more. Back at Twelve Acres they dug deep holes and stumped the still-green saplings into the ground, bending and lashing them together using hemp, a cord made from plant fiber, to create the dome-shaped wetu frame 25 feet in diameter and 14 feet high, and the longhouse that was just as high and about 40 feet long. The lean-to, also framed of cedar, was covered with bark. The intent was to eventually cover the longhouse and wetu structures. A well had been dug, but electricity was needed to operate a pump that would bring water to the garden and provide lighting in the evenings for social gatherings and even a powwow. Allan, as Selectman Maxim, had plans to seek state funding to finish the village and develop a nature trail.[*]

By all accounts, the men engaged in the project took great pride in the effort, and the progress was swift.

"It was museum-quality," recalled Martin "Bruzzy" Hendricks, who was among those who worked on the project. "The way the longhouse was built, the wetu, the farm and garden tower, the picnic area, the fire pit — it was really a nice place . . . . It was something we enjoyed. It was something we were proud of."

The new Tribal Council had been successful securing federal Indian education funding, initially to help tribal students do better in school. In 1976 those funds were extended to allow for a summer program featuring activities to inspire the Wampanoag children to enhance their awareness of their culture. The summer camp began in mid-July, and the village was made available for the group to use as a base. Enthusiasm for the program was high, with more than 60 tribal children enrolled. Morning sessions were established for younger children, ages 5 to 10, and in the afternoons the focus shifted to the children up to age 15. Even while the village

---

[*] Mead, Jim, "Outdoor exhibits show Wampanoag early existence," *Cape Cod Summer Times*, August 8, 1976.

was not complete, it served as an inspiration to the children who were learning crafts, including beadwork, basket making and even the art of making a drum as they held sessions there. They were also instructed in traditional songs and dances.*

A large tent was erected on the site for the education program to store supplies for crafts and activities and was shared with the men working on the village for their materials and equipment. The education director applied for and was granted a permit by the town to allow some of the men to camp on the site each night to provide security. Typically a few of the men would sleep in the tent.

The village construction and summer program for the children were truly multigenerational efforts that became a source of overall tribal pride. Some even suggested the annual powwow celebrated in early July on Collins' Lot be moved to the site of the village construction. While that idea wasn't fully embraced, the Tribe was looking forward to the possibility that it could happen in the future when the village was complete. It certainly didn't stop tours of folks who did attend the powwow that summer from wandering over to admire the work being done.

An impromptu feast

And so it was decided to plan an event to celebrate the efforts of those building the village and the children who had been so dedicated to their cultural education. It was an impromptu feast organized in a few days, but word spread quickly throughout the Tribe of a gathering at Twelve Acres on the afternoon of July 28.

---

*Blake-Lopes, Dawn, Indian Education Summer Program, Report from the Director, 1976.

Everyone was to come and contribute whatever he or she could. It was an atmosphere of organized chaos.

"Guys went off in different directions and said, well, OK, we'll get some corn," recalled Brad Lopes. "Some of the guys went off hunting. Some of the guys went off to the bay."

Billy recalled that some went off to a farm near Camp Edwards, the Air Force base. "They went up to Veg Acres and got some corn right outta the field," he laughed, referring to the custom of appropriating vegetables they knew would never get harvested. "It was the stuff that would just get tilled back into the ground come the fall."

"We went fin fishing; we were picking mussels; we went quahogging," said Earl "Chiefy" Mills Jr. "We were preparing food, we were cooking and we were all pitching in getting firewood."

The event came together organically, and the Tribe and friends turned out in great numbers.

"I was sitting by the fire," Ramona Peters recalled, "and there were some clam cakes being made by Derek Mills, and I was waiting for them to be ready and just taking it all in. There were a lot of people there."

Throughout it all the sound of the drum, so centrally important to bringing people together, was as constant as the heartbeats of the people assembled.

A perfect storm

The weather could not have been more favorable for the Mashpee Wampanoag Powwow, held on the July Fourth weekend in 1976. Not just any Independence Day, it was also significant as the nation's bicentennial, bringing throngs of visitors to Cape Cod. The three-day powwow was blessed with sunny and clear days and comfortably warm temperatures. Attendance both by tourists and participants made the cultural celebration on Collins' Lot memorable as one of the most jubilant and successful in many years. Tribe members from the very young to the elderly were fully engaged — from dancing in fancy new regalia to singing at the Tribe's new drum. Food and crafts were abundant. Guest dancers, singers and vendors represented tribes up and down the Eastern Seaboard, and even some Western nations.

Across from Collins' Lot at the American Legion Hall, adults were grooving to the jukebox and taps flowed into the evening until "last call" urged folks home. On the pond, young people had their own extended celebrations that likely included unsanctioned Wild Irish Rose and skinny-dipping for some, and budding courtships for others, as the occasion offered an opportunity for intertribal dating. Many marriages that link the Wampanoag to Narragansett to Pequot to Nipmuc to Mohican and so on sprang from the tradition of young people meeting at Native American gatherings like the powwow.

But amid the reunions, elated spirits and joyful noise of pow-wow, there was discernible tension in Mashpee. Certainly not all newcomers, but enough, were uneasy with the Tribe's growing sense of entitlement. And among Tribe members and leadership were fears that the character of the village that had been the last bastion of their ancestral homeland was falling victim to the fast pace of development.

Tribal Council President Russell "Fast Turtle" Peters' tone to a local newspaper reporter may have hinted at the Tribe's displeasure. The reporter asked the Tribal leader if the Wampanoag were celebrating the country's 200th birthday during their powwow.[*]

---

[*]Moore, Milton, staff writer, "Indians are cold-shouldering the Bicentennial," *Cape Cod Times*, July 4, 1976.

"My feeling is it's not our birthday," Peters said. "We were here first, and in the 200 years following the Declaration of Independence we haven't made out very well."

Post-powwow, the revelry typically lost steam in the days following the closing ceremony — but not so in 1976. Between the educational program and the ongoing village construction at Twelve Acres, the celebrating became more regular and extended into the nights, often including drumming and singing. Whether they knew it or not, those drummers were in the eye of a perfect storm of social, cultural and political controversy. Their celebrated sound of tradition was rippling across Mashpee Pond to the ears of those who perceived the beat of the drum as a threat.

The first sign that the new establishment had had enough occurred on the 25th of July when a number of young Tribe members and friends were gathered on Mashpee Pond. A call was made to Mashpee police registering a noise complaint. According to newspaper accounts, Sgt. Albert Gonsalves, perceived among the Wampanoag to be notoriously antagonistic, responded twice to the pond.

"He had a bossy attitude," Earl "Chiefy" Mills Jr. recalled of Sgt. Gonsalves. It was something the Native community was not used to — in particular the young people. "He brought a lot of negative energy and rubbed people the wrong way . . . . He liked telling people what to do and in a demanding way that wasn't well-received."

It was just about midnight Saturday when the sergeant ordered the group to "disperse." It was standard police jargon, but the way he regularly barked the word at the young people encouraged more defiance than cooperation.

They mocked him: "Disperse my ass!"

Sgt. Gonsalves whipped around to see who had made the offensive remark.

That night Gonsalves and other Mashpee police officers returned a second time before the young people finally began to leave the pond in various directions toward home. Some, using the path that cut through Twelve Acres, discovered a group of strangers had pitched a tent in the village. One of the teens confronted the campers, suggesting they might want to camp elsewhere. That led to a confrontation in which the teen was attacked by a camper and cut with a knife. Blood flowing from his head, the young man ran down the path toward the fire barn.

At that moment Chiefy was with a group of tribal men crossing Collins' Lot in the direction of the fire station. He recalls seeing young Lawrence "Larry" Balbuena emerging from the woodland path, covered in blood.

"It looked a lot worse than it was," Chiefy said, "but it was pretty scary and got us pumped up."

Before racing up the hill, one of the men ran into the fire barn to get medical attention for Larry from the on-duty firefighters, who also practiced general first aid. He unwittingly initiated the return of the already agitated bully sergeant when the firefighter used the new emergency switchboard to call for an ambulance. Chiefy and the others ran up to Twelve Acres, where they confronted the camper who had attacked Larry. Chiefy recalls the man being afraid, defensive and threatening as the Mashpee men invaded the clearing. Everyone ran in different directions.

This drama was unfolding just as the young people were in the process of "dispersing." At the same time the Legion Hall was closing. A large crowd of curious and concerned folks began to congregate in the parking lot just as several Mashpee police cars pulled in.

Sgt. Gonsalves barked the order to "disperse!" According to a news account he "was answered with a hurled rock, about the size of a baseball, which bounced off his back and against the cruiser, leaving a dent in the car."

Mutual aid was called from Falmouth and Sandwich, and ultimately eight people were arrested, six men and two women — four adults and four juveniles. They included the knife-wielding stranger. [*]

The news account provides none of the details about what instigated the attack on Larry and who was involved. The event was described as a "fracas" and a "melee" in a buildup of what was to come.

In reality, said Chiefy, "It was an isolated incident."

A rude awakening

Three days after the "fracas" and the attack on Larry, as the community feast was coming to an end, sunset offered little relief from the heat of the day and hardly a breeze cut the humid air. But there was a collective sense of satisfaction, and many folks remained at the pond well into the night. On the hill at Twelve Acres a goodly group of Tribe members gathered.

"It was a festive atmosphere, for sure," Chiefy recalled.

The glow from the fire illuminated a time warp — the village structures, dancers in the shadows. Next to the fire a group of men circled chairs around a drum for a "49." The numerical term refers to a drumming session of social songs during which songs learned from other drums are shared, new ones made up or new verses

---

[*] Staff contributor not noted, "Police from three towns quell fracas in Mashpee," *Falmouth Enterprise*, July 27, 1976.

given to old songs. The songs are never actually counted, but the implication is that the drumming might go on until as many as 49 songs have been sung. The number quickly becomes irrelevant. Important is the coming together, the bond created in sharing what is culturally unique and enriching and inspiring to others, especially the young ones watching in the distance.

In the shadows of the outer circle the Boy watched the men and listened to the drum. The beat was comforting. He wanted to join the men, but his friends were down on the beach talking to girls and skipping stones on the water, which was flat as a sheet of glass.

Evidence of the feast was all about: coolers of leftovers in melting ice, pots of chowder and fritter batter.

The gathering was briefly interrupted when two Mashpee police officers came into the circle responding to a noise complaint, and Chiefy addressed them.

"I don't recall who the officer was at the time," Chiefy said, "but they talked about (us) making too much noise. And at the time there was Mother's Lounge at the other side of the hill in the old Attaquin (hotel), and they used to have loud bands there. In fact, Aunt Del used to complain about that, that she could hear that loud music at night and that it was a disturbance to her. So that was in my head about noise and what constitutes a noise violation. And they didn't stop those bands from playing, and they had the doors open because that little place would get hot in the summertime, and that music would come blaring out, and that was fine — but we are up on the hill singing and that's a problem? I had a problem with that. I recall what I said to him was . . . we're just Mashpee Wampanoags in Mashpee doing what Mashpee Wampanoags are wanting to do, something that is within our own culture, and it shouldn't be a problem . . . if they can put up with that rock 'n' roll at the bottom of the hill, I guess they can put up with a little drumming as well. It was just a little exchange between myself and the officer at the time. He left and I thought that was the end of it. Apparently it wasn't."

Police were leaving when they saw the teens on the beach.

"Disperse!" was shouted.

The teens were as defiant as they were fearless. Keenly aware of every path of escape, they disappeared — but not before a stone was thrown.

The good with the bad

On the night of July 28, 1976, Sgt. Robert Costa was in charge of keeping law and order in Mashpee — no easy task, given the building tensions in the community, the now-retired officer recalled. He is still living in Mashpee, where he began and finished his law enforcement career — a town and community of citizens he genuinely respects and cares deeply about. When he wasn't on duty as a police officer back in the day, he drove the school bus shuttling children to the Davis School in Mashpee or across the town line to Falmouth where Mashpee students attended high school.

"I got to know all the kids that way," he smiled.

Sgt. Costa was well-known in the community as not simply a cop and a bus driver, but also as a neighbor. When he wasn't policing or driving kids to school he engaged socially with town folks.

From his seat at the wheel of the bus he was personally familiar with most of the giddy children as they went excitedly off to school. He could restore order simply by barking out a parent's name and saying, "you don't want me to have to call on them after this ride, do you?" And things would settle down.

In stark contrast, his other job exposed him to a much darker side of the community.

"When I pinned the badge on my chest I knew what came with it," he said. "You take the good with the bad."

Raised in the next town over, Sgt. Costa recalled the startling growth of Cape Cod, Mashpee in particular. Issues once simple and easily resolved became convoluted and challenging. The town had brought in retired Army Col. George Bingham to lead the department with his military precision, but there seemed to be no handbook on the reign of discontent growing in the town.

Things were changing at a dramatic pace. "We felt it," he said. "The Tribe felt it."

The police, he said, were right smack in the middle of all of the tension, a moral compass in a vortex of animosity. While they were charged with being objective enforcers of the law, there were so many gray areas — especially where the paths of tribal tradition crossed over the expectations of new residents bringing in an absolute counterculture.

And while the grumbling among Tribe members was getting louder, police were trying to address a serious problem among local youth drinking and smoking pot and acting out defiantly. Sgt. Costa walked a fine line between bus driver and cop in an effort to inspire better behavior.

"I felt bad for the kids," he said. "They had no place to go, really."

It was a common lament among the Mashpee youth, who were being told to go home from the pond or Collins' Lot or the "Cornah" where they had been used to congregating without offending anyone. The kind of gathering that had been practiced in Mashpee for generations had suddenly become taboo.

"There was a lot of resentment. I could understand it," the sergeant said. But he still had a job to do. He would try to issue warnings, give the heated moments a chance to cool off before taking any kind of official action. He recalled the night of the raid on Twelve Acres no differently.

He came on for his shift at about 11 P.M. Soon after, he said, a call came in from residents across the pond of a noise complaint, and he took a ride to check on things.

"There had to be 100 people down there, adults and minors," he said. "There were open containers of liquor, people dancing in the parking lot, people skinny-dipping."

He recalls telling the group to start heading home and to keep the noise down, but he didn't even get back to headquarters before the radioed bark of more complaints.

"I went back and told them all to go home and that if I had to come back I would be taking people to jail," he said.

At the time there were only three officers assigned to the night shift, so when the third call came in just after midnight Sgt. Costa said he was overwhelmed and called for mutual aid from neighboring towns. He then set up staging areas at Collins' Lot and the town landing and assigned a unit to Lake Avenue, effectively securing the scene. As the duty officer in charge, he remained on

Main Street coordinating the response. He admits he never actually went down to the pond area or made any arrests personally, but he did give the order to arrest anyone still partying in Attaquin Park. Despite not physically being there, he vehemently disputes some of the recollections of witnesses and those who were arrested in the park. There is always another side to the story, he said.

Some things you just never forget

For Frank Wing, the serenity of the small-town life, dirt roads, woodlands and nature trails that surrounded his grandfather's Mashpee home all stoked his anticipation before his annual visits to Cape Cod. It was a stark contrast to the busy city life, traffic and concrete that defined his home in Austin, Texas, where his father was deployed for military service and Frank was raised with his siblings. The grandson of Frank Hicks, a longtime Mashpee selectman and first executive secretary, young Frank spent every summer in Mashpee camped out behind his grandfather's house with his brothers and other cousins. It was something his mother insisted upon to ensure her children maintained a connection to their tribal heritage. The summer of 1976 was no exception.

Though he was just as much a tribal member as the other children, as a summer kid Frank felt like a bit of an outsider to those who were culturally immersed year-round. Still, he enjoyed being in town for the powwow and was fascinated by the tribal life and traditions. There were advantages to being raised in a city, including a great diversity of activities and things to see and experience, but the freedom enjoyed by his Cape Cod cousins was not one of them. Frank's mother was very strict, and the children observed a nightly curfew that had them tucked into bed by 11—even on a warm summer night when there was clearly still a lot going on in Mashpee.

On the night of the raid on Twelve Acres, Frank, who was 15 years old that summer, could hear the sound of the drum.

"My grandfather's house was not that far away," Frank recalled of the Hicks homestead, which was just Down Street of the fire barn and Ockry's Trading Post and within shouting distance of the pond. "Of course, I'm curious, because it's like, wow, I want to check this out."

Sneaking out was certainly forbidden, and he knew doing so meant risking his mother's wrath, "but my curiosity got the best of me."

Frank rolled out of his bunk and tiptoed by his sleeping brothers. He found his way in the darkness to the trail by the town landing and then up to Twelve Acres. When he arrived just to the outskirts of the campsite, he stopped before he could be seen and crouched behind the brush to watch. What he'd hoped to observe was over; the drumming had stopped and a few men were sitting around the campfire in what appeared to be a harmless gathering. He was about to leave when he witnessed the rush of law enforcement on the scene from all angles. He sat stunned in the shadows as the raid quickly escalated.

"They had a fire going, and I remember the fire getting kicked up because people were falling in it and stepping in it. There was a lot of shouting. There was a lot of baton swinging," Frank recalled. "I was actually scared."

The scene was both shocking and confusing to him. "It didn't seem like there was anything to provoke (the cops) to do that. I didn't feel like they (the men at Twelve Acres) were doing anything malicious."

Rather than risk being caught up in it, Frank slipped back into the woods and crawled through the low brush back to his grandfather's yard. Shaking and covered with scratches, he told his brothers what he'd seen. But fearing reprisal from his mother, he swore them to secrecy and never told another soul until he heard about the effort to document the story of the Mashpee Nine.

"It's an incident I hadn't thought about in 40 years," Frank said. "But it was something I just never forgot."

Ramona Peters recalled it was well before midnight; the singers were hoarse and the drumming had ended. Some of the men who had been drumming had crawled into tents and were going to sleep, and a few others, like Billy Pocknett, remained by the fireside talking. It was quiet, and about that time she began walking to her home about a mile up Great Neck Road.

In the pond parking lot, Bruzzy was in the driver's seat of his car. Beside him was a young lady, a date whose anonymity he protects to this day.

Another noise complaint was called in to Mashpee police. Accounts of who sounded the alarm are conflicting. Was it a woman who lived across the pond complaining of the drumming sound traveling across the water, or someone from the Legion Hall less than 50 yards away?* One report accused a bartender at the Legion Hall, who not only denied making the call but also insisted nothing was heard over the din of their own jukebox. At the fire barn next door, all was quiet.

Regardless of who made the call, the report of excessive noise coming from Twelve Acres set into motion a series of actions and

---

* Staff contributor not noted, "10 men arrested, 2 officers hurt in Mashpee fracas," *Cape Cod Times*, July 29, 1976.

reactions perceived to be a grave injustice for group of Wampanoag men, their families and the tribal community.

About a mile north of Lake Avenue on Main Street was the combined Town Hall and community center, in an old USO building. The large room inside was at once a gym, a meeting space, a dance hall and a theater, with a stage and a grand piano. All kinds of gatherings of both an official and social nature, including town meeting and benefit dances and game dinners, were held there. A small wing jutted from the left of the building and housed the Mashpee Police Department, including a reception area, dispatcher's desk, the chief's office and two small jail cells that were rarely used. It was often compared to the fictitious Mayberry department run by Sheriff Andy Griffith in the 1960s television series, then still very popular in reruns. But on the night of July 28 the arsenal of the officers who began gathering there was far more threatening than the one bullet Deputy Barney Fife kept in his breast pocket. They fanned out to strategic locations around Attaquin Park for an unprecedented gathering of law enforcement officers and apparatus from four towns and the State Police barracks in Bourne.* Every available Mashpee officer was summoned — with the remarkable exception of Police Chief George Bingham.

While most of the teens on the beach scattered as soon as they saw headlights coming down Lake Avenue, the raid took the men at Twelve Acres completely by surprise.

"There was only about a dozen of us left," recalled Larry Balbuena. He said the drumming had finished and the only sounds being made were the hushed tones of men's voices over the crack-

---

* Staff contributor not noted, "8 defendants deny charges in melee with Mashpee Police," *Cape Cod Times,* July 30, 1976.

ling fire. "Next thing I know I see lights and I hear dogs in the woods."

Brad Lopes had just left the fireside moments before and was on the path from Twelve Acres to the Legion parking lot heading home. A police officer from a neighboring town appeared in front of him in full riot gear, including a helmet and shield. Ironically it was someone he knew, someone he'd grown up with. So he greeted him by name and wondered aloud why he was there. (*This officer did speak off the record, confirming critical details of the raid, but asked that his name not be shared.*)

"There was no squad car," Brad said, "just him. I was baffled, then all of the sudden there were cop cars pulling in and cop cars up the road and cop cars everywhere."

Brad was sure something catastrophic had happened, but until that officer advised him he was under arrest, it never occurred to him that he was a target of the raid.

Back at Twelve Acres, sound asleep inside a pup tent, Chiefy was startled awake. He was kicked and shoved, then blinded by lights.

"It was a long day. I was beat. I was tired out. So when they came in the tent and got me, you know, pulled me out of my sleeping bag, I was like, what the heck is going on here? They didn't announce themselves like they do on TV or anything, you just see the helmets and you know it's either aliens or police," he said. "My mind was racing because the way they were dressed and their behavior . . . you wake up and it's like, what the heck? You are dragged up and out and handcuffed and manhandled . . . that's when one of them was saying something about, 'We are getting even for Custer.' That's when all that stuff started. I'm like, for Custer? Those were the Lakota — that had nothing to do with us . . . . Then they started saying more of that kind of stuff, throwing out like Geronimo's name. Those kind of things. I'm like, what in the heck does that have to do with us singing on Twelve Acres?"

Billy remembered an atmosphere charged with hostility as soon as the raid began. "When they came out they had these black riot helmets on with a shield in front, then they had a shield — you thought you were in the movies or something. And they were just coming from everywhere, just whacking, and, geez . . . they said a lot of stuff . . . trying to provoke you . . . if somebody would have tried to fight they probably would have killed them. No one fought back. You were so overwhelmed with police officers — well, you can't fight back. But if somebody had fought back that night, I think they would have killed them."

Being dragged in cuffs from his tent, Chiefy witnessed a surreal scene. "I was just too surprised in the scenery, from pitch black to flashlights in your face, with the light reflecting off of all of their hardware and stuff . . . . It was a shock, from the peaceful quiet of Twelve Acres, you know, crickets, etcetera, to the radio chatter, lights reflecting off of their hardware . . . . You look around and you start seeing some of the other guys, and they are dragging them around, two cops to a guy, and manhandling everybody because they could — and just the sheer numbers of police was — well, I didn't realize there were that many police on Cape Cod, let alone all in one place."

Chiefy's cousin Derek Mills had been asleep in the same tent but bolted out as soon as he heard the dogs. Escaping the raid on a dirt path toward Main Street, he saw a cop coming toward him and was sure he would be caught. He stepped off of the path and just stood there as the cop ran right by him as if he was invisible. He stayed there long enough to hear the sounds of the others being arrested and the campsite being destroyed.

"They didn't need to do that," he said. "None of it."

Still sitting in his parked car in the lot down by the pond with a date, Bruzzy was alarmed to see two officers dragging his friend Sonny Joseph down the hill from Twelve Acres. Sonny was flanked by two cops and was trying to wrench himself free as they held him by each arm.

"All of the sudden I see these bodies coming out of the shadows. I was like — what the . . . ?"

The next thing Bruzzy knew, his car was surrounded by an army of cops decked in riot gear. He still wasn't sure what was going on or how he was involved when one of them came to the driver's side and flung the door open, demanding he get out. Bruzzy was immediately placed under arrest, but was relieved as police released his date, not a tribal member, without incident.

As the number of prisoners exceeded the capacity of the back seat of a squad car, a patrol wagon arrived on the scene and the handcuffed men were shoved inside.

"They just started piling guys into the paddy wagon one after another, smacking the guys with nightsticks," Billy recalled. "They called us all kinds of names. Just terrible stuff."

The men were dumbfounded as they sat in the patrol wagon, bruised and beaten, hands cuffed behind their backs. But the final insult was yet to come.

A dazed Victor "Streaker" Almeida was the last to be arrested. He was shoved but barely able to fit inside the patrol wagon, and his feet hung out, blocking the door. It didn't seem to matter to the cop on the outside.

"The guy slammed the door on his leg, and I said, hey, what are you doing? His leg is in the door. And he slammed the door again on his leg. Some of us got down and grabbed him and pulled him in because the guy would have broke his leg," Billy said. "Next day Streaker couldn't walk."

The doors finally closed, but opened again slightly enough for the cop to slip his hand inside. A long, steady hissing sound followed.

"He took a can of mace and sprayed, and filled the whole back of (the patrol wagon) and then closed that door up. We're like this," Billy said, demonstrating how he rolled over to the man sitting next to him to relieve the burning in his eyes, "and your eyes are watering, your skin is burning . . . ya just kinda wipe your face on him . . . and it was so hot and humid in there, and they stood outside the paddy wagon talking and laughing and joking . . . ya know, let's go! You're gonna lock us up? Let's get us out of here!"

Nine were taken into custody at the Mashpee police station, crammed into two small cells. When police realized a minor, Larry Balbuena, was among them, he was sent home.

"We didn't even get (to make) a phone call," said Billy. And it was impossible to sleep, but after settling into the situation the men made the best of it, joking among each other until the sun came up.

"I remember us getting into our own humor, teasing each other," said Brad. "I remember Sonny getting wise with you" — and here he pointed to Billy, who'd been confined in a cell across from Sonny — "and you said, if I could get over there, Sonny, I'd wring your neck!"

In the morning, several cruisers lined up outside to collect the men and deliver them to the Barnstable District Courthouse.

"Before they took us to court, they didn't even let us splash water on our face," Bruzzy said. "Hair all over, and they handcuffed us, they had one guy facing one way and one guy facing the other way, and that's the way they brought us in."

"Yeah, in a long line," said Billy. "We looked like a chain gang. People were backing away."

Chiefy recalled a woman snatched up her small child at the sight of them, "like the Boston Strangler was on the loose." "Talk about a spectacle," he said. "It was a spectacle. It was intentional. It wasn't fun."

Charged with excessive noisemaking were Willard F. "Billy" Pocknett, 24, of Main Street; Kevin Hicks, 22, of Great Neck Road; Myron E. "Ricky" Hendricks, 19, of Main Street; Victor P. "Streaker" Almeida, 26, of Main Street; Brad Lopes, 22, of Great Neck Road; and Martin E. "Bruzzy" Hendricks, 22, of Main Street.

Also among them, the only nonresident of Mashpee, was Earl H. "Chiefy" Mills Jr., 21, of Jones Road, Falmouth, who was charged with both excessive noisemaking and assault and battery on a police officer (Patrolman Maurice A. Cooper Jr.).

The most serious charges were levied against the eighth man, Harry "Sonny" Joseph, 18, who listed his residence as the Wigwam Motel on Great Neck Road in Mashpee. In addition to excessive noisemaking, he was charged with disorderly conduct, assault and battery on a police officer and threatening to murder a police officer, Patrolman Cooper. Police identified Lincoln Hendricks, 22, of Main Street, Mashpee, as an escaped participant in the "melee" and obtained a warrant for his arrest. He was picked up the next day and arraigned on charges of being disorderly and violating the excessive noise bylaw.[*]

And so there were nine.

---

[*] Staff contributor not noted, "8 defendants deny charges in melee with Mashpee Police," *Cape Cod Times*, July 30, 1976.

At 6 foot 4 inches tall, Selectman Robert Allan Maxim standing inside the longhouse frame on Twelve Acres gives a sense of its size. This photo ran with a feature story about the exhibit published in *The Falmouth Enterprise* in August of 1976. It is one of very few existing images of the village. (Photo courtesy of *The Falmouth Enterprise*)

This sign was designed to represent the community's pride in heritage for the town of Mashpee's centennial in 1970. (Photo courtesy of the Mashpee Historical Commission)

This is the fire barn, as it was commonly called, where firefighter Donald Duarte worked the overnight shift the night of the raid. No longer there today, the building sat midway between Ockry's and the American Legion Hall and directly in front of Twelve Acres. (Photo courtesy of the Mashpee Historical Commission)

Ockry's Trading Post, circa 1970s. The general store was the feature of "the Corner," a common gathering spot stocked with a variety of essentials, from beer, bait and tackle to milk, bread and penny candy. (Photo courtesy of the Mashpee Historical Commission)

Standing in the front row in this May 1975 photo of the Mashpee Police Department are, from left, Chief George Bingham, Deputy Chief Curtis Frye, Sgt. Albert Gonsalves and Sgt. Robert Costa. (Photo courtesy of the Mashpee Historical Commission)

This 1975 photo is of the old USO building that housed the Mashpee Town Hall and the Mashpee Police Station that occupied a small wing flanking the left side of the building. (Photo courtesy of the Mashpee Historical Commission)

Willard F. "Billy" Pocknett, charged with excessive noisemaking. (Photo courtesy of Donnella Pocknett) Billy lives in Mashpee with his wife, Donnella, and works as the facilities director at the Mashpee Wampanoag Tribal Government Center.

Brad Lopes, charged with excessive noisemaking. Brad lives in Mashpee with his wife, Cindy, and works in health care.

Martin "Bruzzy" Hendricks, charged with excessive noisemaking. (Photo courtesy of the Cape Cod Times) Bruzzy is retired from the Mashpee Department of Public Works and lives in Mashpee.

Earl H. "Chiefy" Mills, charged with excessive noisemaking and assault and battery on a police officer. Chiefy works for the U.S. Postal Service delivering mail in Mashpee, where he makes his home.

Lincoln Hendricks, charged with excessive noisemaking and disorderly conduct. Lincoln, who never raised his gun against a person before the raid, now lives in Bellingham, Washington, where he still hunts to sustain his family. (Photo courtesy of Janet Hendricks)

Myron "Ricky" Hendricks, charged with excessive noisemaking. Ricky lives with his wife in Falmouth, Massachusetts, and is a building and grounds maintenance worker for the Tribe.

Harry "Sonny" Joseph, charged with excessive noisemaking, disorderly conduct, assault and battery on a police officer and threatening to murder a police officer. Sonny died in 2010 at the age of 52. (Photo courtesy of June Hendricks)

Victor P. "Streaker" Almeida, charged with excessive noisemaking.
Victor is retired and lives in Hyannis, Massachusetts.

*Camera shy, despite his charm and good looks, Kevin Hicks was
charged with excessive noisemaking. Kevin lives in Mashpee and
is a buildings and grounds maintenance worker for the Tribe.*

A group of young Tribe members stands amid the rubble at Twelve
Acres the day after the raid. From left are Tommy Hendricks, Robert
Peters, Derek Mills, Milteer Hendricks, the Boy, Greg Joseph and Rene
Banks. (Photo courtesy of *The Falmouth Enterprise*)

Some members of the Nine celebrate at a holiday gathering. Top row, left to right: Brad Lopes, Chiefy Mills, Lincoln Hendricks, tribal supporter June Hendricks, Ricky Hendricks (hugged by unidentified girl). Below, left to right; Streaker Almeida, Lew Gurwitz and Sonny Joseph. (Photo courtesy of Ramona Peters)

Lew Gurwitz

Lew speaks at a rally in Washington, D.C., in 1994 to advocate for freedom for Leonard Peltier. (Photo courtesy of Frits Terpstra)

Empty beds

Flora Hendricks woke to an unusually quiet house. Her sons Myron and Martin were typically early risers. It was certainly odd that they weren't already up and about. Flora walked down the hall, poked her head into the bedroom they shared and found it empty, beds not slept in. This put her at immediate unease. Her sons were grown and independent but would have called if they weren't coming home. She thought immediately to call the police station, dreading some unfortunate circumstance but never expecting what she heard from the voice on the other end of the line.

"Yeah, we got 'em," the dispatcher reported.

Flora was relieved they were safe but couldn't imagine how they had wound up in jail. Her sons were good boys. Never got into trouble much, and certainly not with the police. She hopped in the car and drove down Main Street to the station.

Some 300 miles up the coast, on the Penobscot Indian Island Reservation in Old Town, Maine, Shirley Mills got the news her son Chiefy was among those who had been arrested; she felt both shocked and powerless to help him. She and her husband, Sam Sapiel, packed up the van and headed south on Interstate 95 for a worrisome five-hour drive to Mashpee.

"I had to come right back home," Shirley recalled. "My son had never been in any kind of trouble. I knew something was really very wrong."

Back in Mashpee, Flora arrived at the police station and demanded to know why her boys were being held. The dispatcher shuffled papers on his desk until he turned over the official incident report, which he had, no doubt, just typed. He read aloud the police version of the ambush on Twelve Acres conveyed in the clumsy but authoritative jargon peculiar to police. While a mother is naturally predisposed to defend her child, phrases like "disorderly conduct" and "assault and battery" and "threatening to kill an officer" caused Flora to be highly suspect of the whole story.

"We'll see about that!" she told the officer indignantly, demanding that her sons be released to her custody.

"Can't do that," he answered. "They need to go down the courthouse and go before the judge first. You can get 'em in Barnstable."

"Well I'm not leaving without seeing them," she insisted.

Seeing no harm, the officer led her back through the station. In the hallway she was struck by a foul odor wafting on the humid air, as if someone had tipped an outhouse into a locker room. Some might have turned back, but not Flora—the assault on her senses made her even more determined to see her boys.

Passing an open door to a storage closet, she was alarmed to see the drum the men had been using all summer at their traditional and social gatherings. She asked why it was in there.

"Evidence," the officer told her.

Of what, she thought, that they are Wampanoag?

By the time Flora reached the cells the source of the stench became obvious. It was a feral smell, a smell of willful resistance. The men crammed into the two small cells had the appearance of battle-sapped prisoners of war. It was clear to Flora that the law wanted everyone to see a band of filthy, rancid criminals—but Flora saw instead in her sons and her neighbor's sons just a group of tired, hungry young men in dire need of a bath.

Shirley wouldn't make it to the arraignment, but on the trip south she stopped in Boston, where she had friends at the Boston Indian Council who would be able to offer guidance in such a situation. A group of Native activists at the BIC had started a local chapter of the American Indian Movement to draw attention to just the kind of injustice that was happening in Mashpee. Shirley knew the raid hadn't been simply an attack on her son and the others, but an attack on deeply rooted traditions in Mashpee that were impeding what nonnatives perceived as progress. She knew the response to the incident had far-reaching implications throughout Indian country.

As a mother and a Native woman, Shirley was gearing up for a long battle to clear her son's name and demand justice for all the others. She would not have to do it alone.

"I knew AIM would share our outrage," she said.

The blue view

Sitting at his kitchen table, Sgt. Costa rubbed his brow as if to tease out more decades-old details of the raid. It was so long ago. He started a virtual count of the responding officers as they seemed to click into focus in his mind. "There were our guys . . . then there was one from Barnstable, and Sandwich sent some officers, and Falmouth I know . . . and the sheriff's department . . . maybe about 14 or 15 of us."

He didn't recall that Sgt. Gonsalves and Patrolman Maurice Cooper were there. They were on duty for an earlier shift and should have been home in bed, he said, but news accounts place them at the raid and each of them testified during the trial.

"Well I guess they must have been there," he said.

He admits he didn't see everything from his command post on Main Street but Sgt. Costa witnessed the melee unfolding: people running in all directions, yelling and screaming at police. Rocks were thrown. And while he did not hear law enforcement making racist taunts at the men being arrested, he did hear provocative name-calling aimed at police.

"I could hear people shouting, 'Pigs! Run, pigs!' It was the times, you know. I would let that kind of thing roll off my back, but maybe some of those other guys didn't. I'm sure if something was said to a police officer something was said back."

Sgt. Costa also insisted there was absolutely no riot gear deployed. There were no helmets that weren't standard issue, and certainly no shields. He also denied the regional tactical patrol force was there, "and there was definitely no paddy wagon!"

He stood by his recollections even while they are contrary to undisputed testimony during the trial that referred both to the use of the tactical techniques and the patrol wagon that carried most of the men to jail.

"I did not call in the tactical force. I only called for mutual aid," he insisted.

When asked if it was possible the tactical force had come as part of the sheriff's department response, he said no. They didn't bring riot gear.

Because he did not make any arrests himself, Sgt. Costa was not called upon to testify and has no memory of the trial itself. He does recall that the community became very defensive — mothers in particular refused to believe that any of their children would behave so badly. They lashed out at police as bullies and made the police the target of their rage.

Bottom line: Sgt. Costa believes there was a lot of partying going on that night in Attaquin Park and the response was justified. He does, however, point to a major lack of communication that may have resulted in the arrests of the men on Twelve Acres becoming an unintended consequence of the raid.

"We only learned after the fact that a permit was issued for them to camp there," he said. "The town issued a permit, but nobody ever told the police department."

Dawn breaks on disaster

The following morning Dawn Blake-Lopes got an early morning call from Bernadine Pocknett. Bernadine was frantic.

"You got to get down to Twelve Acres right away!" Bernadine told her.

The two women had been conducting the summer camp on the site for tribal children that summer. Dawn was the education director and Bernadine was her assistant. Dawn raced down to Twelve Acres and could hardly believe what she was seeing. The village site where the men had worked all summer, where the children enjoyed cultural lessons and making crafts, and where the whole community had turned out the day before to celebrate their achievements, was in ruin. The tents were destroyed, tables overturned and pots of food dumped on the ground. Even a baby's cradle left in a tent for Bernadine's granddaughter to nap in while the children learned was tossed about like trash. It looked to Dawn as if a bomb had gone off.

"Everything we had worked for the whole summer was destroyed," Dawn said. "I just started to cry. I knew our men could not have done that. They would never have destroyed something they took so much pride in."

Before cleaning up, Dawn and Bernadine took photos to document the damage. They used a Polaroid camera that had been issued to the summer camp to take pictures of the activities. The modern marvel of photography would hum as it spewed the self-developing film in front of captivated children who watched as images emerged right before their eyes. But that morning there were no giddy children to witness the exposure of what Dawn was certain was a crime scene. So certain was she that she backed up the Polaroid evidence by taking another group of pictures with a standard camera.

"Something told me that I should get another set of those photos," Dawn said.

Later that day, when Selectman Allan Maxim toured the site the women had largely cleaned up, Allan asked if he could use the photos as evidence of the extent of the damage. Dawn gave him the Polaroid images to give to police, but said nothing of the roll of film they would send out to be developed.

A stacked deck

If the raid on Twelve Acres was intended to shock the community, police exceeded their goal. Mashpee locals, the men arrested and even new folks in town had never expected that kind of extreme show of force. And for the nine men arrested, the idea that they could fight the charges and win was at least initially doubtful for some of them. How would they, with limited means, go up against a virtual law enforcement army and a newly appointed district attorney who was among the "good old boys" of the new brand of Mashpee politics? Before becoming the Barnstable County District Attorney, Philip Rollins had sat on the Mashpee Board of Selectmen. If there was a deck stacked against them, Rollins was on top.

But it didn't take long before the Wampanoag community rallied behind the accused men and a campaign was born to "Free the Mashpee Nine." Meetings were held in kitchens and parlors, and the momentum swelled from Up Street to Down Street. There would be justice for the Mashpee Nine.

After the "melee"

The day after the raid a local newspaper reporter found a group of young tribal members at Twelve Acres aghast at the condition of the site — the tent flattened and ripped apart, the food table over-turned, the quahog fritter batter dumped on the ground. The young people insisted there was no call for such force and destruction of property. According to the article published in *The Falmouth Enterprise* the day after the raid, "The sum of their story is this: That they were partying and dancing, that the police came and told them to quiet down and that many of the group left, that when police returned all was quiet. Those remaining, they said, were sleeping or sitting quietly by the campfire when the police began busting heads."

Lincoln Hendricks, one of the nine arrested, agreed the show of force had been completely unprovoked. "They had no call busting us," he said. "All was quiet."

Mashpee police were just as quick to defend their actions.

Police Chief George Bingham did his best to downplay the frenzy that was building around the incident, telling a reporter it was just a case of young people deciding "to raise hell again."[*]

While he was privately outraged that his officers had taken such extreme actions, and without advising him, when he was on a planned out-of-town trip, Chief Bingham was not about to

---

[*] Staff contributor not noted, "Young folk deny provocation when Mashpee cops move in," *Falmouth Enterprise*, July 30, 1976.

throw his men under the bus. The retired Army colonel, who died in 2000, led his department with the strict discipline that came from more than 30 years of military service. He was a physically imposing man, with a tall stature and broad chest that gave him a commanding presence to match his bellowing voice. His uniform, always impeccable, was accompanied by a tobacco pipe hanging from his lip, which he would occasionally draw on, causing a puff of smoke to float over his head like a thought bubble. But anyone wanting to know his thoughts on the raid conducted without his authorization would have to have been in his kitchen, where he vented to his wife, the very same Amelia Bingham who procured the federal grant for the Twelve Acres village — the woman selectmen had removed as director of the Mashpee Wampanoag Museum. Beyond that, his disappointment would be an internal matter.

"We were on vacation in Florida," Amelia Bingham recalled. She said her husband never left town without leaving information on where he could be contacted in the event of that kind of emergency. When they returned just after the raid and discovered how the matter of the noise violation on Twelve Acres was handled, "he was very upset."

Regardless of whether protocol was followed, according to police accounts, things in Mashpee had gotten completely out of control. During the incident earlier in the week, Sgt. Gonsalves had complained that a rock had been thrown at him, and that another had struck his cruiser.

The *Cape Cod Times* evening edition published news of the raid on the very same day, citing a police report that said Sgt. Gonsalves and another officer, Maurice Cooper, were taken to Falmouth Hospital, where they were treated for injuries sustained in what they called a rock-throwing melee, in which Sgt. Gonsalves' cruiser took another hit.

The police report also indicated that the initial call of a noise complaint was made at 12:20 A.M. from the fire station; however, when questioned later, no one from the fire barn admitted to making a call. Sgt. Robert Costa and Patrolman Cooper were dispatched to the scene and reportedly encountered 30 to 50 people in the wooded area behind the fire station. After issuing the order to "disperse," the officers left.

Then, at 12:30 A.M., another call was made to police, this time from the American Legion Hall right next to the fire station, where a complaint was made of rocks being thrown at the building.[*] (This statement was later disputed by the Legion Hall staff.) It was those back-to-back calls of disturbance, along with the rock throwing, that inspired the dramatic assembly of mutual aid from Falmouth, Sandwich, Barnstable and the State Police. That they came ready with tactical weapons and gear suggests a level of readiness that would have required more than 10 minutes.

According to the news story, a command post at the Town Hall parking lot served as a staging area where police officers gathered for instructions before descending upon Twelve Acres at 1 A.M. with orders to arrest anyone still on the scene.

While police reports of both incidents featured stones being thrown, no stone thrower was ever identified or charged with such an act.

Several surviving officers who engaged in the action were located in the attempt to pin down the events of that night, but none has agreed to provide a statement for the record. One officer, retired from another Cape department, did speak candidly about his role

---

[*] Staff contributor not noted, "10 men arrested, 2 officers hurt in Mashpee fracas," *Cape Cod Times*, July 29, 1976.

providing mutual aid to Mashpee for what he was told was a "riot," but he declined to be identified.

That officer said he arrived in the center of town near the fire station as the raid on Twelve Acres in Attaquin Park was in full swing. He was assigned to manage the scene as it was evolving in the Legion parking lot. He said instructions were coming from the "command center," which he believed was at the Mashpee police headquarters. He was told not to make any arrests, but to keep order. He was also warned to stay out of the wooded area and off of the trails because "the Indians were hiding in tunnels and caves and might jump out and attack."

Community outrage

In the days following the raid on Twelve Acres, the reaction of the Wampanoag community went from stunned to outraged over perceived acts of police brutality.

"Everyone was just overwhelmed. We didn't really know what to make of all that," recalled Shirley Mills, who was in Maine when she got the news and rushed home to be with her son Chiefy. "None of my children had ever been arrested before."

Tribal members were also in an uproar about the unrealistic and unfair curfew of 9 P.M. on all town property, including Mashpee Pond and Twelve Acres, and the apparent target on the backs of tribal youths. The curfew had been established after the July 25 late night confrontation between youth and police.

Representing tribal parents, Tribal Councilwoman Hannah Averett requested a public hearing with selectmen and police. On the Tuesday following the raid, nearly 100 townsfolk packed the

Town Hall meeting room to condemn the actions of police and demand answers.

Born and raised in Mashpee, Tribal Council President Russell Peters said in all of his life he had never seen anything enrage his community to that degree and intensity. He was not alone.

His niece Ramona said the bullying by police "never happened before." "That's new to Mashpee," she said.

Tribal Chief Earl Mills Sr. called the police action "an irresponsible, irrational act."

Several young Tribe members gave consistent testimony of aggressive and abusive treatment by police. On the night of the raid on Twelve Acres, Lincoln Hendricks said, he saw Sonny Joseph running with his hands over his head as an officer wielding a nightstick chased him.

But while police were the focus of the outrage, none of the officers who had engaged in the raid was in attendance. Chief Bingham showed up with police reports from two of his officers, each of which the crowd found to lack credibility in the absence of the officers who had compiled them — the only ones who could reasonably respond to questions.

"Why aren't they here?" asked Tribe member Randolph Peters Sr., who was both brother-in-law to the police chief and a special police officer for the Mashpee department. He had not participated in the raid. The meeting erupted in applause and cheering.

Then Chief Bingham's other brother-in-law chimed in. "Were you there?" asked Tribal Council President Russell Peters.

The police chief was clearly antagonized by his wife's brothers, but stopped short of admitting that the lack of an advisory from his rank and file was probably intentional. "If I had been called, I would have been there, dammit!" he answered.

While members of the community pointed to a clear pattern of racial bias in the department, the police reports laid blame squarely on the Mashpee youths and their lack of regard or respect for authority.

This theory was challenged again and again by Tribe members in the room who felt they had been treated unfairly and were being singled out for being Native Americans. One young woman, 16-year-old Valerie Jonas, had been walking home on the night of the initial "fracas" on July 25 and said she had been taken into custody for little else. Sgt. Gonsalves told her anyone found walking the streets was to be picked up. Valerie was jailed in Falmouth, as there was no accommodation for female prisoners in Mashpee, and was never given an opportunity to call her worried parents. Valerie's mother, Margaret Jonas, was outraged and confronted Sgt. Gonsalves after the incident, but found him to be unapologetic and arrogant, offering only "Tell it to the judge!" as a resolution.

The hearing also became a platform to vent about Tribe members being passed over for town jobs. "It's Mr. Charlie who gets the jobs," said Delscena Hendricks, a matriarch of one of the largest tribal families. Not nearly as innocuous as "Gosh," "Mr. Charlie" was a more cynical expression among Tribe folk in referencing the newcomers running the town. The moniker was an allusion to a white man named Charlie Collins who operated a general store directly across from Ockry's and was seen as a competitor to the Native-owned business.

The officers' reports also tried to imply racism on the part of Tribe members toward the police, accusing Chiefy of calling one of the officers a "white honky" as he was taken into custody.

Incredulous, Chiefy, who studied four years of Latin in high school and was entering his third year of college, said he would never have used the term "white" to further define a "honky."

Chiefy also commented during the meeting that he never learned the identity of his arresting officer. When he asked for his name and badge number, Chiefy was told to shut up: "You don't need to know."

The meeting ended with the assembly of a committee consisting of Chief Bingham; Tribal Council President Peters; Mrs. Averett, representing the Tribe's parent committee; and tribal member John Peters, also a brother-in-law to the police chief. The committee met with Mashpee selectmen directly following the meeting, with the first order of business to dispense with the 9 P.M. curfew.*

But the committee also wanted the town to address incidents of police bullying and police brutality on July 25 and July 29. Petitions were submitted for the removal of Sgts. Gonsalves and Costa, the two Mashpee officers tribal youths seemed to be most at odds with.

Sgt. Albert Gonsalves retired from the Mashpee Police Department in 1990. He died in 1998. On August 13, 1976, The Falmouth Enterprise *published the following letter from Sgt. Gonsalves in response to community reaction to the police action on July 25 and the raid on Twelve Acres in the early morning hours of July 29.*

POLICEMAN REPLIES
Editor of The Enterprise:
I wish to comment on the references to me which appeared in The Enterprise *on Aug 8.* The Enterprise *article contained a number of direct and indirect quotes of accusations which were made by members of Mashpee's indigenous population who were opposed to the enforcement of certain state and local*

---

* Staff contributor not noted, "Aroused gathering in Mashpee assails behavior of police in two incidents," *Falmouth Enterprise*, August 6, 1976.

laws as they relate to Mashpee natives. Three of the allegations which were printed relate to my activities.

One Mashpee woman accused me of drawing my service revolver on a "young child." The young lady partially recanted when questioned by a selectmen (sic) but still managed to create the impression that I was the aggressor in the incident. The woman failed to mention that I was the only officer present; that I was facing a group of twenty to thirty youths who were bombarding me with rocks, bottles and cans; and that even then I did not unholster my weapon until after I was struck and injured by a large rock and a Boston-area man was advancing towards me with an upraised tire iron threatening to "crack my skull." How many of my critics would have waited so long before taking defensive action?

A second woman is quoted as having said that I told her to "tell it to the Judge" when she requested information about her son's arrest. The woman in question apparently neglected to mention that I had fully informed her of the charges and circumstances of her son's arrest. When the propriety of the arrest was challenged, I advised the lady to consult an attorney about the possibility of raising a legal objection in court. I felt my refusal to discuss the legal aspects of the case was prudent and proper given the adversary nature of our legal system.

Finally, a Mashpee man is quoted as having said that he overheard me directing another police officer to take down the tent. The Enterprise failed to note that Mashpee has an anti-tent bylaw similar to those on the books in other Cape towns. With the exception of children in backyard play tents, it is routine procedure to arrest people who are tenting in Mashpee without a permit. The tent is usually seized as evidence.

In the incident to which The Enterprise made reference,

it could not be determined at the time who owned the tent. As a result, no complaints were sought for violation of the anti-tent bylaw. In all other respects the matter was handled routinely. The tenant (sic) was left at the scene disassembled, but otherwise in the same condition that it had been in when I arrived.

It is unfortunate that the parents who showed up to so vigorously defend their children's actions are unwilling to devote the same amount of energy monitoring their children's activities. When a hearing is called to discuss police treatment of juveniles, parents show up en masse. By contrast, groups of thirty to forty youths can roam around the Route 130 area until two or 3 o'clock in the morning and not a single parent will call to ask if the police have seen the child.

Albert R. Gonsalves
Sergeant
Mashpee police department

While an investigation conducted by selectmen came up with conflicting accounts of both incidents, the board made a decision not to decide.

"We could talk for six months and not get all the facts," Selectman Kevin O'Connell said, recommending the matter be turned over to the office of the Cape and Islands district attorney.

Selectman Maxim agreed, saying "there would always be doubt if the selectmen made a ruling."*

---

* Staff contributor not noted, "Ask DA to investigate disruptions in Mashpee," *Falmouth Enterprise*, August 13, 1976.

And no one would dispute a district attorney's ruling, added Benway, the selectmen's chairman — especially one handed down by Mr. Charlie himself, former Mashpee selectman and newly appointed DA Philip Rollins.

As town leaders deflected responsibility for determining whether police had used excessive force, Tribe members began to organize a campaign to defend the men arrested.

They met in tribal homes, made buttons and planned fundraisers. When Billy Pocknett's wife, Donnella, opened a bank account, the cause had to be named. And that is how the young men officially became known as the Mashpee Nine.

"We had a lot of support," Billy recalled. "The whole Tribe was behind us."

But not the DA. By the end of September, after interviewing 40 people, the DA issued a report exonerating police of any wrongdoing on the night of July 28 and into the early morning hours of July 29. The report cited public drinking on the beach after hours and defiance of police by those asked to "disperse," particularly on July 25. On July 29, the DA concluded, police were within their rights to bring dogs held on leashes and found no evidence that dogs had been let loose on citizens, as claimed in the complaint. The report also noted an anti-noise bylaw after 10 P.M., an anti-tenting bylaw, and a law forbidding people from being on town-owned land after midnight. Last, the DA found that the people tenting on Twelve Acres did have a permit and were within their rights to be there, but because police were unaware of the permit, police were within their rights to raid the campsite.[*]

---

[*] Staff contributor not noted, "Attaquin Park party: what the DA found," *Falmouth Enterprise*, September 21, 1976.

Tribe makes a bold move

One month after the Mashpee Nine were arrested, the Mashpee Wampanoag Tribal Council filed a land claim action for all the land in Mashpee, based on the 1790 Non-Intercourse Act, a law meant to protect Indian tribes from land grabs.* The lawsuit had been in the planning for months, so the timing was coincidental. While the two legal actions, the land suit and the case against the Mashpee Nine, had a profound impact on the Tribe and community, they were separate, one being a civil action and the other criminal.

The land suit dropped like a bomb on Mashpee, clouding the title of every deed in town. Developers, stunned, were stopped in their tracks. Banks refused to grant mortgages for any property in Mashpee. The building boom went bust.

While the Tribal Council had its hands full managing the precedent-setting lawsuit, which was grabbing national media attention, the grass-roots organization of tribal members and friends was determined to expose the law enforcement injustice occurring in their community and clear the names of each of the Mashpee Nine.

With all of the controversy surrounding the Tribe and the town, the ongoing investigation by the office of the Barnstable County District Attorney into a pattern of police brutality within the Mashpee Police Department, and the land claim action, the trial of the Mashpee Nine was delayed.

(The Mashpee Wampanoag land suit would drag on through 1978, ending with a confusing and devastating decision by federal Judge Walter Skinner that essentially found the Wampanoag lacked

---

* Baker, Kitty, "Tribe sues for Mashpee land based on 1790 protection act," *Cape Cod Times*, August 27, 1976.

the tribal status to sue the town. It would take 30 years to resolve the Tribe's petition for federal acknowledgment, which was finally granted in 2007. By that time, much of the land the tribe sought had been developed.)

By September Chiefy had returned to the University of Massachusetts in Amherst, prepared to come home whenever the case of the Mashpee Nine came up on the court docket. At school he received support from an old friend, Peter d'Errico, a Yale-educated attorney who practiced law for a time among the Navajo and also represented members of other Western tribes caught up in a legal system he felt did not treat them fairly.

The frustration he experienced had led Peter early in the 1970s to UMass, where he established the Native Legal Studies Program. Believing he could be more effective as an educator, he turned his attention to the classroom. As a law professor and activist he introduced the student body to the American Indian Movement (AIM), a group that provided a national voice for Native activism not contained within the civil rights movement.

"Having an academic position gave me a platform; it gave me the ability to bring (AIM) and give them platforms," Peter said, dropping the names of AIM legends: "Dennis Banks, Russell Means, I had them come into class, meet with students, give lectures. John Trudell, another really important figure . . . so people who were active with that American Indian Movement were intersecting with what was happening here at UMass."

While Chiefy was not his student, the two had become acquainted when Peter made his initial tour of tribal communities in the Northeast.

Peter recalled meeting Chiefy, a teenager at the time, on his first trip to Mashpee, when the myth that no Indians remained east of the Mississippi was completely dispelled for the law professor.

"I can remember going into a house in Mashpee where there was a ceremony of some sort .... There was a drum, there was singing of some sort .... I came into that house — it was crowded, [a] packed event — and somehow I got moved into the room where the drum was, and there was dancing. This is part of confirming to me, this is actually authentic, there is no playacting here," Peter recalled. "One of the people I met was Chiefy Mills."

Peter was impressed that Chiefy was a very traditional young man, thoughtful, composed and by all means polite and respectful — certainly not the kind of person Peter suspected would commit a violent crime against a police officer. When he learned about the case of the Mashpee Nine, Peter urged Chiefy to seek help from AIM.

Soon after the start of the fall semester, Vernon Bellecourt, a founding AIM leader, was scheduled to speak at neighboring Smith College. Peter and Chiefy attended. There, Peter introduced Chiefy to his old friend and colleague Lew Gurwitz, a Cambridge-based attorney who worked with Peter defending tribes in the West. Unlike Peter, Lew preferred the courtroom and became a legendary defender of AIM cases and indigenous land rights cases.

Born and raised in Winthrop, Massachusetts, with a practice in Cambridge, Lew surprisingly had never heard of the sleepy little Cape Cod village of Mashpee, nor the Wampanoag, until meeting Chiefy. But the story of the Mashpee Nine fueled his passion for justice.

Lew made the trip with Chiefy to meet the Mashpee Nine and hear their story and, without a second thought, agreed to defend the men, who clearly weren't financially equipped to pay him.

He did have one condition, Chiefy recalled. Lew recognized instantly the significance of the case and knew it was about more than just the nine men wrongfully and brutally arrested. He would defend them, not simply the charges against those nine men, but their right to cultural and spiritual expression on their land. Win or lose, their battle was for cultural justice that belonged to the Mashpee Wampanoag Tribe. It was easy enough for the men to agree to Lew's condition, because in many ways it was how they had always endured as a tribal community.

The Mashpee Nine defense committee barely had enough money to cover court fees when Lew took them on. It hardly mattered. Often for little more than a hot meal, a warm bed and some gas money, Lew was in town interviewing witnesses, gathering documents and preparing the case.

An imposing man, broad and tall, with shoulder-length dark hair streaked with gray, he was powerful both in his presence and his intellect, but his smile was disarming. Lew was always casually dressed in blue jeans and flannel shirts, wearing his signature pair of cowboy boots with an elaborate snakeskin design. And then there was the car, his iconic late-model blue Saab.

"Not sure how he fit himself into it," Billy laughed, remembering the car and how Lew could never sneak into town unnoticed. "People would say, 'Lew's back!'"

In order to effectively represent the Wampanoag men, Lew had to immerse himself among the Wampanoag. The men and their families probably had no idea what a skilled defense attorney he was as he sat around kitchen tables drinking coffee and eating stuffed quahogs. He seemed like a regular guy and quickly became part of the community, something Peter attributes to Lew's willingness to offer his help for little in return.

"Lew was a lawyer who could represent people with technical skill, but he also had the emotional, personal understanding at a consciousness level and heart level of what his client was going through, where his clients were coming from," said Peter, who helped Lew on the Mashpee Nine case remotely from Amherst by preparing briefs. "Lew was plugged in to the community and to the people in a way that I thought — this is authentic in both directions — both his legal talent and his personal rootedness, if you want to call it that. I felt a definite bond that way in terms of Lew, and I could see why he was so important in the places he had worked, why he was trusted. There was [a] time when he would be out in some part of the country where these people didn't have any money that he was to represent, so they would hold a bake sale and Lew would live out of that car or sleep on somebody's floor. He was willing to sacrifice his own personal comfort in order to do that work. So he was a very impressive person in that way."

Lew was a regular guest in Shirley Mills' home, where he became so much more than a defender. "We established a friendship that lasted many years," she said.

Lew's willingness to sacrifice his own comforts, along with his sincere and unwavering belief in the Mashpee Nine's innocence, were critical, as Dawn recalled. Some of the men, not all, had past experience with the legal system that left them doubtful they would ever get justice; some even considered entering a guilty plea.

"I asked them, why would you do that? Why would you plead guilty when you did nothing wrong?" Dawn said. "But there was this sense of defeat, the way they just shrugged their shoulders and said, 'There is no sense fighting them, we are never gonna win, that's just the way it is, Dawn.' I couldn't accept it."

But for them, probation and a fine were a small price to pay to avoid being harassed by the same cops when everything was over.

The cut-and-run phenomenon was something Peter d'Errico was very familiar with, especially in Indian country, where "the heat is always on the person that is the defendant, whose life is being disrupted, who is the one who is looking down the end of the road and saying . . . 'Well, if I defend myself, this whole apparatus that is against me and doesn't understand me is going to have it in for me and make things worse for me, so I'd rather just disappear.' That's very common in these situations."

Dawn recalls that Lew gave the Nine hope and convinced them it was at least possible to win.

"Lew was able, because he was living among people there, staying there, and trusted . . . to say, 'This is an opportunity to change how the law looks at you. Sure, it's going to mean work, sure you are going to have to take the heat, but I'm right there with you' — and he was clearly not there just to make money," Peter said. "The defendants who were going to take the heat, who were going to take the risk, knew that they were not being milked for some kind of fee, that this guy was sleeping on a couch somewhere and that he was working for the food he was getting every day. There was no question that this guy was there out of some sense of commitment, of doing this thing because it needed to be done, if there was going to be any progress in the law treating people differently."

During an initial hearing that Lew understood to be a discovery hearing, he encountered the first obstacle — one he was certain was intentional in the district attorney's push for a speedy trial to clear the police of any wrongdoing. Assistant DA Alan Green brought in several police officers to give their testimony. The DA claimed the defense had been notified about the witnesses, but Lew had never received notification and was not prepared to cross-examine them. Lew asked for a postponement but Green objected, as his office had already paid the officers to be in court on their day off. Judge Dennis L. Collari agreed to a postponement, but only if the defense paid the officers on the spot.

"Lew pulled me aside," Dawn recalled. "He wasn't ready and they knew it. They were trying to pull a fast one."

Going forward on that day would seriously compromise the

defense, Lew told her. But the Mashpee Nine defense fund was tapped after paying filing fees.

"I just took out my checkbook," said Dawn. "It just had to be done."

That check bought Lew the much-needed time to depose witnesses and prepare the defendants. Ultimately the depositions of several law enforcement officers became key to the defense. Studying them all carefully, Lew discovered many inconsistencies and outright discrepancies. It also became clear that officers within the Mashpee department and several other officers who responded to the raid from other departments had been part of an organized militia of police representing nearly every Cape Cod town and the State Police.

And the nine defendants were able to practice their testimony and improve their confidence to tell their story in a room where, for several of them, their level of comfort had been prejudiced by previous experience. Lew also taught them how to present themselves in a courtroom. It wasn't necessary for them to force themselves into an unnatural costume like a suit and tie so long as they brought their integrity. They would hear many things during the course of the trial they would disagree with, and even find hurtful, he instructed them, but they must make no disruptions as he made their case. They needed to trust that he would answer each accusation in due time.

Mashpee Nine on trial

On December 27 of 1976, Lew marched confidently into the Barnstable District Courthouse wearing his snakeskin cowboy boots and a suit he'd gotten from a thrift store. Behind him, in stark contrast to the men dragged in five months earlier in shackles, the Mashpee Nine sat cleanly groomed and neatly dressed. Some wore plaid flannel tucked into belted jeans; others wore handmade shirts of calico fabric adorned with brightly colored ribbons hanging front and back, as had become the popular Native custom. Long hair was tied back with folded bandanna headbands. Denim jackets had AIM logo patches sewn on in solidarity with the American Indian Movement.

About 120 spectators filled the courtroom, most in support of the Mashpee Nine, including family and members of both the Tribe and AIM — too many Natives in one room for authorities, who expressed concern that some kind of demonstration was planned. But it never occurred.*

The case was heard by Judge Dennis L. Collari, a Plymouth County justice, who may have been chosen to avoid the appearance of a conflict; a local justice might be seen as being influenced by the sensational story and the politics around the case of the Nine at the same time the Tribe's land claim suit was heading to federal court in Boston. The idea that the Wampanoag were actually asking for land back was a captivating story dominating headlines both on the Cape and more broadly — in *The Boston Globe* and *Herald* papers and on the national television news. Despite the land claim drama, the case of the Mashpee Nine became one of the most high-profile cases to have been heard in the Barnstable County court.

While Lew represented the Wampanoag men, Harry "Sonny" Joseph had retained his own attorney, Stephen Rappaport of Falmouth. Rappaport recalls meeting with Lew on several occasions

---

*Staff contributor not noted, "Trial begins for 9 charged in violating Mashpee law," *Cape Cod Times*, December 28, 1976.

and being very impressed with his skill and approach. Rappaport admittedly argued Sonny's case in Lew's shadow.

"I followed his lead," recalled Rappaport, who left the legal profession some 20 years ago and is now a newspaper editor in Ellsworth, Maine. "He was an amazing courtroom litigator."

He likened Lew's technique to the approach taken by Alan Ladd in his portrayal of Shane, the iconic Western hero. Holding up his hand, Rappaport demonstrated how the gunslinger removed his glove, slowly, one finger at a time, before he delivered his justice.

"That was Lew, laying his case, methodically and strategically. He was incredible to watch."

Lew's first motion before Judge Collari on behalf of the Mashpee Nine was to establish a cultural correction to a judicial custom. The idea that the accused Mashpee Wampanoag men would be asked to swear on a Bible to tell the truth, the whole truth and nothing but the truth would have been a hollow gesture. Instead, Lew argued, the traditional medicine pipe should replace the book. His motion was granted.

Peter d'Errico recalls why that was such an important victory at the start of the trial. Being handed a Bible to swear upon that only the truth would pass your lips has always been a problem for Native people. The origin dates back to the authority granted by the papal bulls, writings of the pope used to subjugate Native people. In particular, the Doctrine of Discovery issued by Pope Alexander VI in 1493 authorized every European explorer to take land and freedom from indigenous people around the world in the name of the church.

"That became part of U.S. law in the early 19th century, when the U.S. Supreme Court used the Doctrine of Christian Discovery to say Indians don't own any land because they are not Christian, and the pope said that only the Christians can own the land," Peter explained. "They were being handed a Bible, which is actually a symbol of what has been oppressive and what has been aggressive against them . . . . To my knowledge, that whole process to get from the Bible to the pipe had never happened before in a Massachusetts court, and may never have happened anywhere in a U.S. court."

For Dawn, having the pipe replace the Bible was an early sign that things might go well for the Nine.

"It was so moving and meaningful," she said. "It was a turning point. I knew we had a difficult path, but I knew the judge would be fair."

On the first day of testimony Mashpee officers Sgt. Albert Gonsalves and Patrolman Maurice Cooper claimed that 45 to 50 people had been in Attaquin Park and the adjoining Twelve Acres site when they arrived in the early morning of July 29. Cooper called it a disorderly "ceremony." He said there were "people yelling and screaming and drums beating."

The prosecution rested after hearing from just those two witnesses, apparently confident of the open-and-shut nature of cases hinged on the integrity of law enforcement.

Lew did not call any witnesses that day but promised to prove the defendants acted within their constitutional rights of free speech and free assembly and, most critically, that their religious and spiritual rights had been violated by police.

The Warriors

The hearing continued on December 29, when Lew scored another early victory for the defense as charges against brothers Martin "Bruzzy" and Myron "Ricky" Hendricks were dropped. Lew argued that Alan Green, a Hyannis attorney representing the district attorney, provided no evidence that the brothers had been involved in any behavior in violation of the town's anti-noise bylaw. Bruzzy, sitting in a car with a young lady, had certainly not committed a crime — especially when the young lady walked away without being charged. Similarly, Ricky could not be placed at the scene of a disturbance of any kind — a disturbance that Lew was out to prove had never occurred in the first place.

The judge agreed and also reduced the charge against Sonny, finding Assistant DA Green had provided no evidence that Sonny had threatened to murder officer Cooper.[*]

The DA's case was so weak, Lew argued, that charges should simply be dropped on all of the men. But the judge disagreed, and the trial proceeded. Lew's first witness, education director Dawn Blake-Lopes, testified to the horrific nature of the damage done to the program property.

To support her testimony, Lew requested that police produce the Polaroid photos Dawn had turned over in July. They were lost. Lew shook his head, then opened a file on the table in front of him and produced the second set of images Dawn and Bernadine had kept secretly. The pictures of strewn food, overturned chairs and tables, torn tents and otherwise ruined educational materials were introduced into evidence.

Lew also called firefighter Donald Duarte to the stand. Firefighter Duarte had been on duty that night at the station, hardly 50 yards from Twelve Acres. He said he'd heard no drumming or loud noises all night.

Despite having their charges dropped, the Hendricks brothers continued to attend every hearing. There was also growing support

---

[*] Staff contributor not noted, "Judge clears brothers of Mashpee charges," *Cape Cod Times*, December 30, 1976.

for the Mashpee Nine, not only from their Mashpee tribal family and friends, but also from tribal supporters around New England. Shirley Mills recalls vanloads of Native people coming from Maine and New Hampshire. Dawn was comforted each time she saw the courtroom filled with Native people. While they couldn't be certain what impact it was having on Judge Collari, there was no question it bolstered the spirits of the Nine.

The Boy returned to school in the fall distracted and disillusioned. He cut class more consistently than attending. His behavior became more and more delinquent, as smoking pot and partying gave him far more satisfaction. While some of his friends attended the trial of the Mashpee Nine, the Boy avoided it — partly because he had already developed an uneasy association with juvenile court in that same building, but also because of a sense of guilt he was stuffing in his already overpacked emotional baggage.

Since 1970 the Cape Cod Regional Tactical Patrol Force had been practicing crowd-control techniques, training dogs and collecting munitions, specialized equipment and other apparatus, much of which had been surplus from the Vietnam War effort. Clearly hours, if not days, had gone into the planning for the raid on the Mashpee Nine.

When the trial continued just after the New Year on January

10, 1977, Lew called Brad Lopes and Lincoln Hendricks to the stand. Each gave extensive testimony of his activity preceding his arrest.*

But it was Lew's cross-examination of police that provided some of the most telling testimony, ripe with contradictions of their own reports and of the testimony of other officers who responded in the raid.

Lew kept officer Cooper on the stand for several hours. Cooper claimed that he had been assaulted by Chiefy, but could not remember many other key details about the raid. In fact, his standard response to Lew's questioning, "I don't recall," was repeated so many times that Lew kept count and, in his closing arguments, remarked that Cooper had repeated the phrase more than 60 times.

Cooper did say he remembered hearing noise when he arrived at Twelve Acres for the raid. Lew pressed him to describe the noise. It was a yelling, chanting noise, Cooper said. So Lew asked him what it sounded like. Cooper responded with a squeal, and the courtroom erupted in laughter.

As Lew's strategy began to unfold, it became clear to the borrowed justice that the trial would not be swift. With a full schedule in Plymouth, Collari began scheduling dates in Barnstable on Saturdays.

On the last Saturday in March the trial continued. Assistant DA Green called four witnesses who were residents of Lakewood Drive, about a quarter of a mile across Mashpee Pond from Attaquin Park. In contrast to the testimony of the firefighter who had been sitting in the station hardly 50 yards away, the Lakewood Drive residents claimed to have heard "screaming and yelling and loud drumming."

---

* Staff contributor not noted, "Judge again postpones Mashpee noise case," *Cape Cod Times,* January 11, 1977.

All seven of the remaining defendants had an opportunity to testify to the nature of the activities just before the raid and the brutal nature of their arrest. Chiefy testified to the ritualistic nature of the drumming activity that had become quite regular at Twelve Acres; the location was a sacred place for the Wampanoag, he testified. He said the drumming had both social and spiritual significance to the Tribe. He also testified of racially insensitive remarks made to him by the Sandwich officer who had sprayed him with mace and arrested him. Chiefy said that while he refused to identify himself, the officer claimed to be one of "Custer's descendants, determined to get even."*

Despite Lew's assertions that the defendants were subjects of repeated harassment by police because they were Native, up to that point the prosecution had been in denial that race was an issue. But on that Saturday it became clear that the DA would need to play his own race card. During the defendants' testimony about the arrests, the term "paddy wagon" was used repeatedly to describe the vehicle that transported them to the police station.

Assistant DA Green objected, saying, "Others have told me they consider this in the nature of a racial slur."

Lew, who was earning a reputation for dogged tenacity before Judge Collari, took that opportunity to show his hospitable nature. "There is no intention to cast slurs on anyone," he said. And from that time forward he used the term "police van" when referring to the defendants' mode of transportation to the police station.

Judge Collari closed that Saturday hearing with the expectation that closing arguments would be heard at the next court date, set

---

*Walsh, Donald, staff writer, "Defendants claim tribal rites at trial," *Cape Cod Times,* March 27, 1977.

for April 30, and a ruling issued — unless, of course, a surprise witness was called.

After one more postponement, final arguments were heard on Saturday, May 28, with one more witness called to the stand — the surprise Judge Collari may have been anticipating as he came to know Lew's flair for drama. Lew called Mashpee Patrolman Lawrence Frye to the stand. Officer Frye said he was among the first to have arrived on the scene of the raid just after midnight on July 29, and heard no drums. He also "could not recall any screaming or loud noises."[*]

Lew then made his closing argument to Judge Collari featuring the significance of the tribal spiritual rites of the Wampanoag men. In a passionate summary he explained the sacred tradition of the drum and how critically important it was to the defendants and to the next generation of Wampanoag. The evidence, Lew said, proved that the men on Twelve Acres in the early morning of July 29, 1976, were not engaging in an activity in violation of an anti-noise bylaw, and that the contingent of law enforcement that responded that night was unnecessarily excessive as it raided the defendants' legally permitted campsite, employing violent and abusive measures to arrest them.

Denying that there was any religious or spiritual significance to the gathering after midnight, DA Green rebutted by saying, "These men remained behind to raise a little hell and were engaged in a breach of the peace of the entire neighborhood."

Judge Collari wasted no time in issuing a ruling.

"Not guilty," he proclaimed with a bang of his gavel. His ruling

---

[*] Walsh, Donald, staff writer, "Mashpee men innocent in noise trial," *Cape Cod Times*, May 29, 1977.

applied to all nine. The date was May 28, 1977 — 10 months after the raid and five months after the opening of the trial.

The certitude of the judge's pronouncement left even Tribe members stunned. "I remember he said, 'None of you should have been brought in here in the first place,'" Shirley Mills recalled.

The shouts of joy among the spectators could be heard throughout the courthouse, but the nine acquitted men and their attorney stood quietly and respectfully as the judge exited the courtroom. They reacted just as Lew had taught them: pridefully. There was no need to gloat in victory. There would be celebrating to come, but in that moment, they were warriors.

Four decades later, some who hear this story for the first time wonder why it ends with Judge Collari's verdict. Why was no civil suit ever filed against the police?

The answer is consistent with the Nine's courtroom demeanor upon hearing the verdict: Eager to move on with their lives, the exonerated men simply never considered turning the justice system on law enforcement.

"We won," said Bruzzy, who was content to have his reputation and integrity restored. "What more could you ask for?"

And, as Lew expressed it, the victory wasn't just for the Nine.

The not guilty verdict restored honor to the Mashpee Wampanoag. It fueled pride in their heritage and a fresh passion for tribal traditions that inspired the formation of a drum group called the Young Bloods. They are old men now, passing their drumbeaters to a new generation of traditional singers. You just can't put a price on that, Chiefy said.

While there may have been merit for a civil claim against the police, "there was no value in that for us," he said.

Several attempts were made to contact surviving law enforcement officers named in this case, including Maurice Cooper, now retired and living in Florida. All, with the exception of Sgt. Robert Costa, declined to comment for the record on the 1976 raid on Twelve Acres resulting in the arrest of the Mashpee Nine.

There had to be a reason

Despite Collari's ruling, there will always be those who sympathize with law enforcement and believe there had to be a reason for so many officers to come down on that gathering of Wampanoag men on that fateful night in July of 1976.

And perhaps there was. Lew did identify the Cape Cod Regional Tactical Patrol Force as being instrumental in the raid on the Mashpee Nine, but, ironically, he missed one critical piece of evidence that might have provided a clue to the fraternity's motivation — perhaps because no one was looking for it, or perhaps because it was buried on Page 5 of *The Falmouth Enterprise* three weeks before the raid on the Mashpee Nine. Whatever the reason, it was missed, not uncovered until four decades later. It provides a possible answer to the "why" in this case of colossal cultural injustice.

On the last day of June in 1976, 30 members of the tactical squad assembled in all their glory before a gathering of Cape Cod police chiefs and the Barnstable County Commissioners. They performed a 10-minute display of crowd-control techniques, including the line, diagonal and wedge formations. It was apparently something they had been practicing since forming the squad in 1970 — the key word being *practicing*.

While Cape Cod overall was certainly experiencing the growing pains that go along with becoming a world-class vacation destination, the region was still very sparsely populated and rural. The need for such a well-armored and organized riot control force was being called into question after Barnstable County Sheriff John J. Bowes requested an additional $5,000 for equipment. At that June 30 meeting, County Commissioner Edward Crowell balked at the idea.

According to a *Falmouth Enterprise* news brief, "In its six years, the force has been called four times, for two peace marches, a nude-in in Truro and a Provincetown rock concert, although it wasn't used any time."

FALMOUTH ENTERPRISE
JULY 6, 1976

Tactical Force Shows Its Stuff

Thirty police officers forming the Cape Cod Regional Tactical Patrol Force demonstrated crowd control techniques to Cape police chiefs and county commissioners Wednesday.

In a 10-minute display at the Barnstable County Police academy the officers, from the majority of Cape towns, marched and demonstrated three formations—the line, diagonal and wedge, used in crowd control.

The tactical squad, which practices regularly at the academy, has recently been the subject of controversy when Sheriff John J. Bowes asked county commissioners to provide $5,000 to purchase squad equipment.

Two commissioners approved the expenditure but Commissioner Edward Crowell voted no, calling the force unnecessary. The state Committee on Counties later withdrew the appropriation on the recommendation of State Rep. Bernard Wilber, who insisted the force wasn't needed on the Cape.

In its six years, the force has been called four times, for two peace marches, a nude-in in Truro and a Provincetown rock concert, although it wasn't used any time.

Unfortunately, with that track record, even the finely executed militaristic marching display failed to convince Crowell the group was necessary. Upon his recommendation, the funding was denied.

Did the Cape Cod Regional Tactical Patrol Force need to justify its existence by responding to an actual riot with actual arrests? Perhaps. But it seems it missed a perfect opportunity less than a week after the county commissioner's rebuke when thousands flocked to Falmouth Heights to celebrate the bicentennial with reckless abandon.

According to a report in *The Falmouth Enterprise* on July 6, in the early hours of Monday, July 5, Falmouth Police Sgt. Donald L. Price estimated a crowd of about 2,000 revelers roaming the Heights, drinking heavily and setting off fireworks with no intention of going home.

"It was one helluva mess," the Falmouth paper quoted him saying.

Price assembled every ready patrolman and squad car to quell the crowd, which responded with a "brick-and-bottle throwing donnybrook," the paper noted. Price said the rest of the town was left vulnerable, as it took every vehicle at the department's disposal to respond and arrest 120 people.[*] The report made no mention of mutual aid or the engagement of the trained and ready Cape Cod Regional Tactical Patrol Force.

By the 1970s Falmouth Heights had become a well-known summer retreat from South Boston, earning the beachfront collective of cottages, inns, bars, restaurants and nightclubs the nickname "Irish Riviera." It is safe to assume the massive gathering of Indepen-

---

[*] Staff contributor not noted, "120 young people arrested as disorder sweeps Heights," *Falmouth Enterprise*, July 6, 1976.

dence Day Weekend revelers in Falmouth that night were largely white. Three weeks later events in Mashpee featuring Native youth would be described in terms far harsher than "donnybrook" — from fracas to melee to all-out riot. Were the Wampanoag low-hanging fruit for the task force to earn its merit?

One can only speculate. But 40 years later, it is hardly lost on anyone that law enforcement continues to target poor minority communities at a far greater rate and with far more lethal force than when responding to incidents in upper-class and affluent white communities.

From Sanford to Ferguson to Baltimore, a pattern of racial bias and excessive force by police has been undeniably pervasive in underprivileged, nonwhite communities across the country. So much so that our first African-American president, determined not to make race a cornerstone of his presidency, nevertheless spoke out on race relations as he had never done before.

In the wake of the Justice Department's finding on Ferguson, President Barack Obama did not mince words when he said what had happened there had not been an aberration.

"What we saw was that the Ferguson Police Department, in conjunction with the municipality, saw traffic stops, arrests, tickets as a revenue generator as opposed to serving the community and that it systematically was biased against African-Americans," Obama remarked. "It was an oppressive and abusive situation."

Seeds of that same systematic bias, only then against Native Americans, were being sown in Mashpee four decades earlier when the tactical patrol force, needing to generate a different kind of revenue, bypassed a "donnybrook" of white lads for a contrived Mashpee Indian melee.

It could have ended a lot differently, recalls Billy Pocknett.

"They were trying to provoke us," he said. "They wanted us to fight back — and if we did, I'm pretty sure somebody would have ended up dead."

Ambushed and outnumbered, they saw the writing on the wall. They would retreat to fight another day, and win like warriors.

Epilogue — The Boy becomes a Warrior

The 2015 Mashpee Wampanoag Powwow became a perfect opportunity to collect interviews from those who had recollections about the case of the Mashpee Nine. The Boy had become a Man, and he grinned sheepishly when asked if he wanted to tell his story.

"You don't want to know my story," he said. "You don't want to know."

"Sure I do," I said. "I want to know everyone's story. Good, bad or indifferent, it puts the whole story into context."

"You don't want to know mine," he repeated, and he walked away.

Early the next day I saw him from a distance on the dry and dusty fairgrounds path. As we walked toward each other, I could see he was shaking his head in a way one does when disappointed about something. It was already quite hot; he was sweating as if he had been running, and looked as if he had hardly slept — and certainly not showered. I was happy to see him. He gave me a sad smile as he leaned in to tell me his story.

"I ain't told nobody this in 39 years," he started. "It was all my fault. It was my fault they got arrested. When the cops came and told us to git, I told 'em, you git! I told 'em, this is our fucking land! You git off it!

Then I picked up a stone and I threw it. It broke the cruiser window. Then I ran."

Tears cut a streak through the dust on his puffy cheeks, and he heaved himself into my arms and sobbed. The burden of four decades of guilt melted over me.

It's hard to describe the kind of medicine that was transferred from the Man to me in that moment, but I was at once heartbroken, grateful and hopeful.

Heartbroken for all of his suffering. Grateful he'd found the courage to surrender it. And hopeful that he would find recovery in sharing his story.

It began almost instantly.

"It wasn't your fault," I told him, "You were a boy. A boy who said and acted in a way that everyone else in the Tribe wanted to."

There was so much more to the story than a stone thrown. So much more that he never had an opportunity to know until the documentary project began to take shape in the Mashpee Wampanoag community. Reviving the story forced the Man to unpack his emotional baggage and learn the truth about what a warrior he really was.

One of the first things he wanted to do was tell the Nine the truth, to apologize for what he believed had caused them to have to endure such a horrible experience.

Part of me was sure they must have already known — that the secret he'd kept for all those years really wasn't a secret. This is Mashpee! Secrets are impossible to keep in Mashpee!

But, in fact, Chiefy was just as stunned by the revelation as I was.

It explained a lot.

It explained, at least in part, the Boy's reckless youth and life-time of addiction. It validated Sgt. Gonsalves' claim. It provided important context for this story.

And perhaps most important, it released the Man from the bonds of guilt that had tortured him for nearly 40 years. His conscience finally unencumbered, immediately upon telling me his story he felt physically lighter. It was as if he had given me the stone.

What an incredible gift.

Afterword

This is a story that would have ended quite differently if not for the dedication of one brave, compassionate and dedicated man: Lewis S. Gurwitz.

A social justice warrior for indigenous people across this nation and Canada, Lew died in August of 1994 at the age of 56.

At the time of his death he was visiting First Nations people of Edmonton, Canada, where he had agreed to take on an environmental case. He was conducting his brand of due diligence, getting to know the people first, dancing around their drum, when he suddenly fell lifeless in the circle.

He had suffered a heart attack and was instantly gone.

"He died with his boots on, doing what he loved," his friend Peter d'Errico said.

His loss was felt throughout Indian country, where he had camped on many couches, fought many battles, shared in many ceremonies, and made many friends.

After he defended the Mashpee Nine, Lew returned to Mashpee again and again as both honored guest and legal warrior.

He defended us when our hunting and fishing rights were challenged. And when tribal member David Hendricks was gunned down by a Mashpee police officer in 1988, Lew became the lead attorney representing the David C. Hendricks Committee for Human Rights.

His terms never changed. His services were rendered for the meager funds raised and the offerings of a grateful community.

"When I got the news I was just devastated," said Shirley Mills, who frequently had Lew as a guest in her home. "We lost a true friend."

He was a man with so great a presence, so giving a spirit, so large in our hearts, that he can never truly leave us. Lew's memory is evoked annually during the Mashpee Wampanoag Ball in an award given to a non-tribal member who displays unselfish dedication as a tribal friend.

A poem written by the late wife of Chief Vernon "Silent Drum" Lopez shortly after the raid on Twelve Acres in 1976.

The Night of July 28th

The sun was slowing sinking in the west,
A time when the spirits cease to rest.
The word was passed by young and old,
A mini Pow Wow they would hold.
You bring the fish, and I the spuds;
The girls, they'll wear their dancing duds.
So the clams were dug, and the wood was split,
All was ready by the time the girls had the fire lit.
The Drum! The Drum! Did Chiefy Bring the Drum?

One by one they came, as if the Spirit drew a map,
To a place their ancestors had swung a mighty bat.
At first the beats were like a jive,
And then by some unseen hand, they came alive.
The dancers rose both young and old,
All would dance to better their Soul.
On that hilltop, in the dead of night,
A song arose that gave a fright.
The Drum! The Drum! Oh, Chiefy beat the Drum!

A chant was carried across the lake, and through the trees,
For all to know, the Wampanoag Spirit was at ease.
The eerie sound was heard both far and near,
To some with pride, while others fear.
Thanks, they gave to Mother Earth and Grandma Moon,
Quick another chant, another Boom!
Their native Blood raced through each vein,
The call of the wild, they heard again.
The Wamp! The Wamp! Who said the Wamp was dead?

The light from the fire would show you all,
That no one meant to harm or gall.
But up the hill that silent crew,
Came a menace wearing blue.
The dogs were loosed, the children ran,
Oh! Will our young ones ever dance again?
That night of nights which brought delight,
And even Gill put up a fight.
The Wamp! The Wamp! Who said the Wamp was dead?

— *Mary Lopez*
For the Wampanoag of 1976

About the Author

Paula Peters is a modern traditional Wampanoag woman. She is a mother, daughter, wife, student, writer and, now, author.

A former journalist at the *Cape Cod Times* for more than a decade, she has produced several scholarly papers on Wampanoag history, driven by a passion for preserving the story of her people from the tribal perspective. Her work has also appeared in magazines and online publications and is included in *Dawnland Voices: An Anthology of Indigenous Writing from New England*.

Mashpee Nine: A Story of Cultural Justice is her first book.

She lives with her family in Mashpee, Massachusetts, in a multigenerational household.